Belated Travelers

Post-Contemporary Interventions

Series Editors:

Stanley Fish and Fredric Jameson

BELATED TRAVELERS

Orientalism in the *Age* of Colonial Dissolution

Ali Behdad

DUKE UNIVERSITY PRESS   Durham and London 1994

Second printing, 1999
© 1994 Duke University Press
All rights reserved

Library of Congress Cataloging-in-Publication Data
appear on the last printed page of this book.

Contents

✦

Preface

✸

Many times during my reflections on the beginnings of this intellectual journey, the study of the cultural and political implications of Western representations of "Orientals," the violent memory of one cold autumn night in 1979 has returned to me. While working on a writing assignment in my dormitory room on the campus of a midwestern university in the United States late one night, I was startled by the belligerent voices of two fellow resident students, shouting anti-Iranian slogans at my door. Soon their violent words were accompanied by the sound of darts sinking into my door. Imprisoned and claustrophobic—thus reenacting feelings I had often felt during those 444 days of the hostage crisis—I silently waited, trapped inside my room, until the campus police arrived. During those harrowing minutes, well before I had learned much about Orientalism, I could not but feel scapegoated by the power of representation and stereotypes that had transformed me into a metonymy of what the Middle East signifies in the collective imaginary of the United States: incomprehensible terrorism and fanaticism. Although I finally managed to repress the terrifying memory of that experience—well after American students had forgotten the hostage crisis—I could not overlook the way my identity as an "Oriental" in the United States had been interpellated by the violence of popular representations of the Middle East and Islam. Thus, through my experience I came to realize early on how, to a large degree, the cultural confrontation between the West and the Middle East is of a discursive nature. It should not be surprising that I later became interested in the genealogy of those representations and tried to understand the history that had helped to construe me as a threatening, threatened Other.

This book emerges from that personal interrogation, and in some ways its writing "exorcises" the violent image-repertoire that has haunted me.

But I have also chosen to preface this volume with that memory to "make real" the crucial effects and consequences of representations of otherness in the West, and to suggest that writing a counterrepresentation, or a genealogical history of Orientalist representation, is not merely a theoretical exercise but a praxis, understood as a creative and self-creating practice through which we act on our histories, our everyday lives, our world, and ourselves. As I write these lines, belatedly, the media and memories of later personal encounters remind me of the continual re-animation of negative representations of the Middle East and Islam in the West today. Thus, this text can only be the beginning, for me, of a long journey. That Orientalism as a Western discourse on the Other continues to operate so powerfully only makes the need for counterrepresentational practices more urgent. The kind of practice this book offers belongs to an oppositional field of discourses that "intend—without necessarily succeeding in implementing—the end of dominating, coercive systems of knowledge," as Edward Said defines them. In the pages that follow I try both to establish a historical knowledge of Orientalism's complexity, by way of situating its cultural hegemony, and to further articulate more effective tactics to oppose its coercive authority. What allows Orientalism to remain such a productive force in (neo)colonial power relations, I argue in this book, is its ability as a dominant discourse to incorporate differing and heterogeneous ideological elements, thus making possible the production of a whole series of hegemonic discursive practices in various epistemological domains. New tactics of oppositionality can be effectively articulated only in a shifting and multiple series of local moves against such global discourses of power, moves that must be antitotalizing, tactical, and against the grain to be effective.

My practice works from a "decentered consciousness" critical of both methodological and discursive consistency. I have studied texts from different domains of representation in nineteenth-century France and Britain to account for the complexities of Orientalism, but without any intention of constructing a unified field of discursive practices or suggesting a topical uniformity among them. In a similar vein, I have used theoretical texts from various "fields" of knowledge—including anthropology, literary theory, history, philosophy, and psychoanalysis—considering them, as Gilles Deleuze has suggested, as "a box of tools" to be used only when they prove useful and only when they add something to other areas of inquiry. Needless to say, my attempt to cross cultural and discursive boundaries has entailed some "exclusions," among which the absence of Islamic intellectual thought produced in the Middle East is perhaps the most obvious. For reasons I would like to explore elsewhere in greater depth, there exists only a small body of works on Orientalism produced in the Middle East itself. Interestingly, the "Middle Eastern" texts I do utilize are the work of diaspora intellectuals, written in French, among them Abdel Malek's "Orientalism en crise," Hichem Djaït's *L'Europe et l'Islam*, and Hassan El Nouty's *Le Proche-Orient dans la littérature française de Nerval à Barrès*. Although important Middle Eastern intellectuals such as Ali Shariati, Jalal All-Ahmad, Abdelrahman el Munif, and Eqbal Ahmad critiqued (neo)-colonial relations of power early on, their privileging of the economic domination of the West over its cultural hegemony left unquestioned the powerful discursive field of European *representations* of the Orient that my project, produced as it is in the West, problematizes. I have tried to address other lacunae in the conclusion of this study by way of suggesting new directions in postcolonial historiography.

Acknowledgments

During the course of working on this project I have benefited from the advice, support, and attention of many teachers, colleagues, and friends. To begin, I express my warm gratitude to Anne Herrman, Domna Stanton, Tobin Siebers, and Stuart McDougal for their helpful comments, criticism, questions, and encouragement. I am also thankful to the stimulating students and colleagues who were a source of great support during my three years at the University of Rochester—especially Janet Wolff, Warren Crichlow, Mieke Bal, Lisa Cartwright, Nick Fabian, Ann Braitwaite, Walid Raad, and Brian Goldfarb. Other friends and teachers I thank for many useful and interesting conversations are Ranu Samantri, Shawn Maurer, Warren Johnson, John Kucich, D. A. Miller, Stephen Greenblatt, Zohereh Sullivan, Nancy Paxton, Evelyne Accad, Paul Viellie, Denise Brahimi, Meaghan Morris, R. Radhakrishnan, and Françoise Lionnet. I owe special thanks to Ken Wissoker and my two anonymous readers for making the publication of this book possible. My immense gratitude also goes to my parents, Hassan Behdad and Fatimeh Oskoui, and the rest of my family for making me feel that regardless of immense distances, I always have a home.

Two fellowships from the University of Michigan allowed me to complete the first draft of this book. Earlier versions of chapters 1, 2, and 4 appeared in French Forum 15.1 (January 1990), *Peuples Méditerranéens* 50 (January–March 1990), and *Victorian Literature and Culture* 20 (Winter 1994), respectively.

And finally, I owe my greatest and most pleasurable debt to two people: Ross Chambers, whose generosity, friendship, and intellectual enthusiasm taught me much beyond Orientalism; and Laura Elisa Pérez, the most wonderful *compañera de viaje*. To them I dedicate this book, with much love.

Introduction:
The Predicaments of Belatedness

❂

This is not a *récit de voyage* but a *discours de voyage*, a "metanarrative" about different kinds of traveling through literary texts, theoretical domains, images, photographs, signs, letters, and traces. Writing is here viewed as a mode of "traveling theory" that involves displacement in time and space: writing about colonialism in a postcolonial era, and writing it in the West.[1] Some postcolonial intellectuals have used the chronotope of travel to reconceptualize the very nature of intellectual practice. Following Edward Said's discussion of writing and displacement, James Clifford, for example, has suggested the return of theory to its etymological root, *theorein*; that is, a "practice of travel and observation, a man sent by the polis to another city to witness a religious ceremony."[2] (Dis)placed in a world of global contacts where communities, economies, and subjectivities constantly cross, theory, he argues, "is no longer naturally 'at home' in the West" (179); it has been destabilized by other locations, contested by other trajectories of subjectivity, and displaced by other forms of knowledge. As a postcolonial practice, this text is therefore conceived as a kind of itinerary mediated by a complex network of diasporic conjunctures, conflicted histories, hybrid identities, and conditions of displacement and transplantation.

This book began as a topical work on the notion of opposition in modern orientalist texts in England and France. As an "amateur traveler" (a tourist?), I began searching for something I unconsciously knew was absent: opposition and counterideologies in a hegemonic discourse. I discovered consciously the *presence* of their *absence*. I found counterdiscursive practices, but they were working within the system as effects of its power relations. Opposition, I began to realize, was not a negative force outside the dominant, but a formative element that mediated the production and maintenance of orientalist power and knowledge. This realization shifted my focus from a topical work on Orientalism to a *belated* postcolonial study of the micropolitics of Europe's desire for the Other and its productive function in the discourse of colonial power.

The kind of cultural critique this text offers is belated in at least two ways. First, genealogically, it comes after the anticolonial responses of Frantz Fanon, Aimé Césaire, Albert Memmi, and other founders of postcolonial discursivity, and it attempts to rework through a kind of philosophical *décalage* our perceptions of the colonial encounter. Oppositional reading, as Louis Althusser has demonstrated, is inescapably late, lagging behind what it hopes to transform and write beyond. Second, historically, the critique of Orientalism this book offers also lags far behind the colonial encounter it addresses, and as such it belongs to an *anamnesiac* order of discourse. But this recognition complicates the status of this work's historicity and raises the question as to what the aims and implications of its writing practice are.

Postcolonial Belatedness

A postcolonial traveling theory such as this is inscribed within a whole field of political practices: the project of postcolonial discursivity as a *belated* philosophy of praxis. Let me elaborate on this critical inscription through a theoretical detour—or perhaps *re-tour?*—through Althusser's belated practice of Marxist philosophy, elaborated in his seminal essay "Lenin and Philosophy."[3] Here, Althusser defines Marxism as a "philosophy of praxis," arguing that this new practice is a kind of *"pratique sauvage,"* which, like Freud's wild analysis, "does not provide the theoretical credentials for its operations and which raises screams from the philosophy of the 'interpretation' of the world which might be called the philosophy of *denegation*. A wild practice, if you will, but what did not begin by being wild?" (65–66). This last rhetorical question provides a theoretical beginning for my reflections on the possibility of postcolonialism as a kind of *pratique sauvage*, a kind of praxis that is a new political theory, coming after the anticolonial responses of Fanon, Césaire, Memmi, and other founders of postcolonial discursivity. While these founders of postcolonial oppositional discourse provided what one may call the "science of anti-imperialism," postcolonial theory today is a new practice of philosophy that politicizes the academic debates about race and gender as it reworks—or more accurately, transforms—the perception of the colonial encounter and opposition to it. But before situating my practice in this field of oppositional knowledge, I want to reflect briefly on Althusser's discussion of the new Marxist philosophy as a traveling theory.

Althusser distinguishes two phases of Marxism, scientific and philosophical, pointing out that Lenin, a figure often marginalized in philosophical discussions, produced a *philosophy* of Marxism that lagged behind Marx's *science* of history. Marxist philosophy necessarily lags behind the science of Marxism because Lenin read Marx *belatedly* to produce a crucial *décalage* (dislocation) in its history—and here Althusser, of course, belatedly reads Lenin's marginalized philosophy to politicize the debates in the Société Française de Philosophie by outlining an interventionist, political philosophy. Reading in each instant is necessarily late, lagging behind what it transforms or writes beyond.

Lenin's reading of the Marxist science of history is not merely an interpretation but a kind of epistemological dislocation that produces a new phase, a new consciousness, a new set of practices—and as such, Althusser claims, it is capable of transforming the material world. Practicing philosophy is, in short, the "consciousness of the ruthless" that divides in order to produce new political practices—and *dividing* here should be understood as a form of political contestation, and not as a kind of disciplinary separation by which the philosophy of interpretation operates. Althusser's emphasis on the necessary *lag* of Marxist philosophy, coming after the science, draws attention to the issue of the belatedness of political philosophy to which my traveling theory belongs; that is, historical hindsight becoming the enabling condition for oppositional theory.

Althusser also insists on the newness of this wild practice, "*new* in that it is no longer that rumination which is no more than the practice of denegation, where philosophy, constantly intervening 'politically' in the disputes in which the real destiny of the science is at stake, between the scientific that they install and the ideology that threatens them" (66). He uses the term *dénégation*, which is not only the psychological notion of denial but also the political attitudes and acts of repudiation, or the action of refutation. Althusser's point about the newness of Lenin's "practice of philosophy" underscores the political consciousness of such a belated— and new by virtue of its belatedness—reading. A belated reading is not an orthodox reiteration or a reapplication of a previous theory; rather, it is an interventionary articulation of a new problematic through the detour— or, perhaps more accurately, retour—of an earlier practice. The belated practice of philosophy is therefore a mode of discursive contestation, and having renounced denegation, this wild practice is consciously political and "*acts according to what it is*" (66). The new practice of philosophy is a "certain investment of politics, a certain continuation of politics, a certain rumination of politics" (37), Althusser insists.

Such a philosophical practice recognizes the limits of its interventionist politics and can only assist in transforming the material world—it can only mediate the possibilities of change—because "it is not theoreticians, scientists or philosophers, nor is it 'men,' who make history—but the 'masses'" (67). In short, new practices act as catalysts that mediate the political struggles of contingent communities—mediation is here the political component of belatedness, of reading *behind*.

Althusser's reflections offer an interesting theoretical space in which to consider postcolonialism as a belated praxis in the academy, for they draw attention to three fundamental components of this new field of knowledge: the wildness of postcolonial consciousness, its belatedness, and the academic context of its formation. Postcolonialism, as a philosophy of praxis, comprises a field of wild practices, *wild* in that their counter-systemic and contestatory stance defies the boundaries of the disciplinary impulse that tries to name and compartmentalize them. Postcolonial counterdisciplinarity depends on a certain historical consciousness that constitutes it as necessarily beyond the boundaries of disciplinary formation; it renounces disciplinary denegation—the depoliticized, divided space of compartmentalized academy—by connecting the separate disciplinary boundaries in alternative ways through critical interventions. The counterdisciplinary position of postcolonialism can therefore be viewed as a practice in negotiation and exchange—both in the ways different modes of knowledge intersect *and* in the ways postcolonial critics negotiate with the academy to mediate new oppositional possibilities; for example, the inclusion of texts and voices previously excluded from various disciplines.

The problematics and politics of postcoloniality demand a counterdisciplinary mode of knowledge to rethink the relations and distinctions between ideology, history, culture, and theory. Because the science of imperialism, as a modern discourse of power, produces a plurality of subject and ideological positions, any critique of such a science can be accomplished only through interdisciplinary praxis. Edward Said, for example, has persistently renounced the disciplinary space of a compartmentalized academy, arguing against the dominant principle in American

universities that "knowledge ought to exist, be sought after and disseminated in a very divided form."⁴ Following Antonio Gramsci and Michel
Foucault, Said argues cogently that the dominant culture in the West
achieves its hegemony by making invisible the "actual affiliations that exist
between the world of ideas and scholarship, on the one hand, and the
world of brute politics, corporate and state power, and military force, on
the other" (136). While universities play a central role in producing the
"experts" and the professional knowledge used by corporate and state
powers, any political discussion of knowledge encounters disciplinary
resistance on campus.⁵ Social and political processes and economic interests are always immanent in the pursuit of knowledge and the production
of power, but the effects of differentiation, separation, and denial render
them opaque. The counterdisciplinary practices of postcolonialism attempt, through their "decentered consciousness," to expose the internal
conditions of these strategies of differentiation. In the place of the dominant will to specialize, Said suggests, "there must be interference, crossing of
borders and obstacles, a determined attempt to generalize exactly at those
points where generalizations seem impossible to make."⁶

Said's own work provides a fascinating example of antidisciplinary practice. In Orientalism,⁷ for example, he demonstrates how Europe's geopolitical awareness of its "exotic" Others was distributed into aesthetic
representations as well as within economic, sociological, anthropological,
historical, and philosophical texts, all of which provided a heterogeneous
discourse of power through which the Orient was colonized. Said describes in great detail how culture becomes a productive site where a
plurality of interests are articulated and brought into contact with the
kinds of military, economic, and political strategies that produce a complex system of domination. Given the multifarious and composite network of power relations, a critique of Orientalism can be produced only
in an interdisciplinary project addressed to a broad-spectrum audience.
As a postcolonial critic, Said therefore situates his work within a plurality
of interests and readers: he addresses his book not only to various university scholars who would benefit from his discussion of the interrelations
between culture, history, and texts but also to policymakers and Orientalists, to present them with their "intellectual genealogy" and question their
false assumptions about the Middle East, as well as to the general public in
the United States and the "Third World," to demonstrate the "strength of
Western cultural discourse" (24). The aim of postcolonial antidisciplinar-
ity is, in short, to expose how seemingly specialized discourses are in

fact linked in ways that allow for the complexities of Western cultural hegemony.

Such a postcolonial critique suggests also an oppositional consciousness to read against the grain. Said describes his goal as a critique of the intellectual genealogy of mainstream studies of the Middle East: his work remembers through archival work what has been historically forgotten. As Homi Bhabha remarks, "Said's work focused the need to quicken the half-light of western history with the *disturbing memory* of its colonial texts that bear witness to the trauma that accompanies the triumphal art of Empire."[8] Postcolonial studies are on the side of memory, their oppositionality a function of *anamnesia*, as they expose the genealogy of oppression and the oppressed, the veiled political economy of colonial powers, the "imaginative geography" that separates the Orient from the Occident, the black from the white. Postcolonial critiques in this sense are the belated return of the repressed, disrupting that structure of colonial amnesia that denied the colonized his or her history. In "Orientalism Reconsidered," Said points out that "what for the most part got left out of Orientalism was precisely the history that resisted its ideological as well as political encroachments, and that repressed or resistant history has returned in various critiques and attacks upon Orientalism, which has uniformly and polemically been represented by these critiques as a science of imperialism."[9] Postcolonial practices are the belated return of the repressed histories of resistance.[10]

Colonial Memory and Postcolonial Anamnesia

Crucial to the understanding of this belated return of the repressed is the notion of temporal difference in the discourses these practices critique. Johannes Fabian, in his powerful *Time and the Other*, describes how the concept of time is a crucial "carrier of significance," defining the unequal relation of self and Other—"primitive" being a temporal concept.[11] In a genealogical approach like Said's, Fabian argues, the epistemological conditions of ethnographic representations of the Other depend on a "persistent and systematic tendency to place the referent(s) of anthropology in a Time other than the present of the producer of anthropological discourse" (31). In other words, the anthropologist, in spite of sharing time with the Other in order to produce the empirical data for his or her research, writes an ethnography that denies the Other coevalness, placing the object in a time other than the Western present. This is accomplished through a whole series of methods and techniques such as unilateral observation of the "natives"; classification of their habits and practices; taxonomic descriptions; uses of maps, charts, and tables to visualize the Other's culture; and so on.

Responding to the denial of coevalness, postcolonial practices are exercises in remembering; they bring into consciousness the repressed time of the Other and work through a demand for coevalness in their belated readings of the science of imperialism. They question the hegemony of taxonomic and allochronic representational strategies of the discourse of power through recourse to the history they were denied. Whereas the discourses of power circumvent the question of history through the uses of cultural relativism or taxonomic approaches, the wild praxes of postcolonialism produce the conditions of coevalness and contemporaneity for dialectical confrontations of cultures through remembering; they demystify the allochronic discourse of power while reclaiming the unrepresented history. These practices recognize that the geopolitics of imperialism had and continues to have its ideological foundations in what Fabian calls "chronopolitics," the politics of time. As the belated return of the repressed histories of resistance, they struggle for recognition of coevalness in their new histories of resistance.

Malek Alloula's provocative rereading of colonial postcards in *The Colonial Harem* is an interesting example of anamnesiac praxes of postcolonial historicity:

> To map out, from under the plethora of images, the obsessive scheme that regulates the totality of the output of this enterprise [i.e., the production of colonial postcards] and endows it with meaning is to force the postcard to reveal what it holds back (the ideology of colonialism) and to expose what is repressed in it (the sexual phantasm).

> Behind this image of Algerian women, probably reproduced in the millions, there is visible the broad outline of one of the figures of the colonial perception of the native. This figure can be essentially defined as the practice of a right of (over)sight that the colonizer arrogates to himself and that is the bearer of multiform violence. The postcard fully partakes in such violence; it extends its effects; it is its accomplished expression, no less efficient for being symbolic.

> A reading of the sort that I propose to undertake would be entirely superfluous if there existed photographic traces of the gaze of the

colonized upon the colonizer. In their absence, that is, in the absence of a confrontation of opposed gazes, I attempt here, *lagging far behind History, to return this immense postcard to its sender*.[12]

Alloula's postcolonial reading of the memories of the colonial encounter inevitability lags far behind history to produce the absent gaze, the unwritten historical text; it is an exercise in remembering, a recourse to a repressed memory that history has swept away, an anamnesia that produces new histories of resistance through speaking about the lack of a returned gaze in the history it tells. Alloula describes his text as a personal "exorcism" that thwarts the desolate gaze of the colonizer. The discursive exorcism situates *The Colonial Harem* as an interventionary political practice empowering the postcolonial with the ability to look back.

Such an anamnesiac practice is the opposite of the nostalgic histories of colonialism that have been and are in vogue today—the colonial nostalgia in films such as *Chocolat, Out of Africa, A Passage to India,* and *Ishtar,* or the nostalgic republications of orientalist works in France. Whereas these amnesiac practices glorify the violent history of colonialism as a utopian time of benignity and exultation, the critical incentive behind postcolonial anamnesia is to counter the nostalgic "forgetfulness" that obscures the genealogy of the science of imperialism, and so allows for its return in new forms. The anamnesiac reading is therefore a symptomatic reading, one that unmasks what the object holds back and exposes the violence it represses in its consciousness. It is, in other words, a *prise de conscience* that fashions itself by bringing into postcolonial consciousness what it finds in the colonial memory.

And yet, to read belatedly the traces of the colonial memory, or to send the card back to a sender who may or may not happen to be there to receive it, does not *necessarily* constitute an oppositional praxis. To be sure, a large number of what claims to be postcolonial reading is belated in a very conventional sense. Produced within the very limits of topical studies such as "Common Wealth" literary studies and Orientalism as a literary topic, these readings do, in fact, lag behind the politics of contemporaneity in their conventional claim to history. A case in point is Sander Gilman's otherwise interesting essay "Black Bodies, White Bodies."[13] On the surface, Gilman's essay embodies everything one expects to see in a postcolonial reading: an interdisciplinary bent, historical consciousness, and anticolonial rhetoric. The essay also accomplishes its task of describing the genealogical connections between the icons of the Hottentot female and the prostitute in the nineteenth century. But Gilman concludes the essay by turning the political into the psychological as he argues that these medical and artistic myths of race and gender are the result of the white man's "internal fear, the fear of loss of power," which he projects into the sexuality of the Other (256). The essay fails to investigate the productive function of racial difference in colonial power, and so leaves out the effects and genealogical connections of such myths in current discourses of race and imperialism. Such topical practices are exercises in what Althusser calls the philosophy of interpretation or the philosophy of denegation, which works through a profound denial of contemporaneity. Not only does Gilman's essay undermine the complexities of the dis-courses of power by relegating them to mere psychological projections of fear, it also circumvents historicity in that it displaces the current politics of race and gender, which has its genealogical roots in the discourses he discusses, into a safe past. For Gilman, history seems to be what is past, forgetting that the critic lives in history, that genealogy is not merely an erudite knowledge of the past but, as Foucault points out, a kind of research activity that "allows us to establish a historical knowledge of struggles and to make use of this knowledge tactically *today*."[14] In other words, postcolonial historiography can be politically meaningful only if it accomplishes a link between past phenomena and present events.

Postcolonial belatedness can be an oppositional praxis only if it main-tains a coeval recognition of its own historicity—its own "worldliness"— and makes use of its historical consciousness to critique the cultural con-ditions that continue to produce unequal relations of power today. With-out such historical consciousness the postcolonial reading of the colonial encounter is at best an informative ethnographic representation of colo-nial violence, and, at worst, a displaced interpretation of archival mate-rials. The postcolonial archival work, in short, ought to restore to the science of colonialism its political significance in the current global set-ting. What would emerge out of such a reading is not a specialized erudite knowledge of Europe's guilty past but the provoking rediscovery of new traces of the past *today*, a recognition that transforms belatedness into a politics of contemporaneity.

Critical Departure

As a political critique of European imperialism's cultural economy, Said's *Orientalism* has been a powerful point of departure for many postcolonial critics—*departure*, in its polysemy, as both a starting point and an act of divergence, of moving away. Not only did this text bring the issue of colonialism to the forefront of the intellectual establishment by critically displaying the ideological underpinnings of the scientific and artistic representation of "otherness" in European thought throughout modern history, it was also one of the seminal books that prompted a shift in the interest of literary and cultural theoreticians from textuality to historicity, from the aesthetic to the political, and from individual receptions to collective responses to literary texts.

In its deconstructive study of Western knowledge about the Other, *Orientalism* has been a vital force in inaugurating a new phase of cultural and literary studies marked by a recognition of the complicity of European knowledge in the history of Western colonialism. Following Foucault's critique of "pure" knowledge, Said demonstrates for the first time that orientalist representations are not " 'natural' depictions of the Orient" but constitute the backbone of "a relationship of power, of domination, of varying degrees of a complex hegemony" between the Occident and the Orient (5, 21). Said uses *Orientalism* to mean several things: whatever anyone who teaches and writes about the Orient does, "a style of thought based upon an ontological and epistemological distinction made between 'the Orient' and . . . 'the Occident' " (2), and the ensemble of institutions dealing with the Orient. Orientalism, he argues, is both a "*distribution of geopolitical awareness*" into every discursive domain and an "*elaboration* not only of a basic geopolitical distinction . . . but also [of] a whole series of 'interests' " (12). In a genealogical historiography that covers almost every kind of orientalist text from Barthélemy d'Herbelot's *Bibliothèque orientale* (1697)—in which Said situates the origin of modern Orientalism—to recent area studies of the Middle East in American universities, Said undertakes the laborious task of describing the systematically "coherent" structure of Orientalism, the essentializing modes of its representations, and the "internal consistency" of its institutional configuration.[15] All of these, he points out, depend for their economy on a tendency to dichotomize "human reality" into us/them, black/white, Occident/Orient.

The strategic purpose of such essentialist distinctions is to create a useful paradigm to justify the appropriation of the Oriental Other. To divide the world into binary oppositions in which the first terms are always privileged is to impose an unequal distribution of power, in this case between the Orient and the Occident, giving the "positional superiority" of the West the status of a "consensus," and "a manner of regular-

ized (or orientalized) writing, vision, and study, dominated by impera-
tives, perspectives, and ideological biases ostensibly suited to the Orient"
(202). Endowed with such an epistemological mastery, the orientalist can
then act as a "judge of the Orient" and as an "egotistic observer" who
represents and appropriates the Oriental Other for the benefit of the
imperial power (103).

Ironically, in denouncing the essentialist and generalizing tendencies of
Orientalism, Said's critical approach repeats these very faults. Significant as
it is, Said's monolithic notion of Orientalism as a purely reductive and
biased discourse of power leaves no room for the possibility of differences among the various modes of orientalist representation and in the
field of its power relations.[16] Although Said makes certain distinctions
among different forms of Orientalism—for example, between academic
or professional and aesthetic or personal discursive practices—he tire-
lessly reiterates his principal argument that "every European, in what he
could say about the Orient, was a racist, an imperialist, and almost totally
ethnocentric" (204). For Said, Orientalism is a "coherent subject matter," a
"closed system" with a "cumulative and corporate identity" to dominate
the East (70, 202).

It is precisely away from such essentialist views of Orientalism that I
wish to travel. Although I agree with Said's compelling argument that
European discourses of the Other are exercises of power that contribute
to the colonial exploitation of the Orient, his insistence on the coherence
and monolithic character of Orientalism seems paradoxically consistent
with the logic of Orientalism/colonialism. To argue that all representations of the Orient are always produced according to the discriminating
strategies of a hegemonic cultural discourse is to remain within the limits
of the old metaphysical binary structure on which the discourse of Orientalism is predicated. The claim that "Orientalism is fundamentally a political doctrine willed over the Orient because the Orient was weaker than
the West" reinscribes itself within the same ideological constraints and
conceptual oppositions that regulate the discourse Said attacks. Indeed,
the formalization of Orientalism as a coherent and stable system of representations unwittingly functions as a reification of unequal power relations between Europe and the Orient. Said's inadequate attention to the
complexities of power relations between the orientalist and the Oriental
makes him reaffirm in a sense an essentialist epistemology that derives its
authority from the dichotomies that it puts forth. Instead of offering an
alternative set of theoretical positions or dissimulating the seemingly reg-

ulated structure of orientalist strategies, Said's postcolonial discourse of victimhood paradoxically positions itself within the confining matrix of identification it strives to subvert and reifies the very distinctions it wants to supersede. *Orientalism* thus uncritically reproduces the stereotypes of the orientalist as the infallible master whose power of representation allows him or her to dominate indisputably the victimized Oriental.

These theoretical limitations in *Orientalism* are the effects of a macro-political historiography that attributes epistemological coherence to discursive formations, constructs a totalizing interpretative framework based on "great men" and "great books," and views power relations in terms of a repressive hypothesis. In formalizing Orientalism's discursive regularities and the dominant system of its ideological constellation, Said's text cannot account for the complexities of its micropractices; that is, the specific but crucial points of its dispersed network of representations that include strategic irregularities, historical discontinuities, and discursive heterogeneity. On the one hand, as Bhabha cogently argues, "there is always, in Said, the suggestion that colonial power and discourse are possessed entirely by the colonizer, which is an historical and theoretical simplification."[17] Foucault's critique of the juridical conception of power that relies on the notion of prohibition cautions us against defining power relations in wholly negative and repressive terms. European discourse and power over the Oriental can continue to function not through the *exclusion* of the latter from the network of power relations but because the Other is strategically placed within their fields. The relations of colonial power are too productive to put the colonized into a position of exteriority with respect to their operational mechanism; nor can these relations be simplified to the point of being reduced to a prohibitive and restrictive function. Rather, European power over the Orient must be understood as a productive and dynamic exchange between the two that makes colonial authority tolerable to those on whom it is being imposed. What makes the exercise of colonial power acceptable to the Oriental is precisely the fact that it has a productive function and that it opens positions that meet his or her desires and needs. No matter how "weak" the Orientals were, would they really have accepted the European colonizers if they were only being dominated and repressed by colonialism?

Finally, Said's insistence on Orientalism's coherency, as Aijaz Ahmad has pointedly remarked, is a consequence of a high humanist tradition that ironically, in an anti-Foucauldian fashion, "trace[s] the origins of this very 'discourse' [i.e., Orientalism], in the conventional form of a continuous

European literary textuality, all the way back to Ancient Greece."[18] Although Ahmad himself relies on a Marxist "grand narrative" marked by continuity and evolutionism, he is on the mark in arguing that Said's historiography assumes a "unified European/Western identity which is at the *origin* of history and has *shaped* this history through its *thought* and its *texts*," and that such a history is "immanent in—and therefore available for reconstruction through—the canon of its *great books*" (167).

This book moves away from such traditional modes of historiography and toward a genealogical understanding of history that treats past discourses and events as discontinuous practices and attempts to grasp the productive effectivity of colonialist power and knowledge by addressing the micropolitics of Europe's relation to its Others.[19] Orientalism, I argue, depends for its economy on a "principle of discontinuity" that makes possible the production of a whole series of discursive practices in various epistemological domains. Different modes of orientalist representations neither constitute a "discursive consistency" nor form equal parts of a monolithic system of "internal reproductions," for they often contradict one another. Difference, ambivalence, and heterogeneity, as Lisa Lowe argues in *Critical Terrains*, are fundamental attributes of orientalist representations, and they allow the possibility of multiplication and dispersion of statements. What gives Orientalism its efficient discursive power, what makes it a productive force in European colonial power, as I will show later, is the all-inclusiveness of its epistemological field and its ability to adapt to and incorporate heterogeneous elements.

Belated Orientalists, Ambivalent Practices

Orientalism's discursive heterogeneity finds its most complex manifestations among the *belated* traveler-writers of the mid- and late nineteenth century. The orientalists of this period undertook an exoticist project marked by an anxiety of coming after what had come before.[20] Traveling in the Orient at a time when the European colonial power structure and the rise of tourism had transformed the exotic referent into the familiar sign of Western hegemony, these orientalists could not help but experience a sense of displacement in time and space, an experience that produced either a sense of disorientation and loss or an obsessive urge to discover an "authentic" Other. Whereas the experience of lateness made orientalists like Gustave Flaubert, Gérard de Nerval, and Isabelle Eberhardt nostalgic about the disappearing Other, and therefore more conscious of Europe's appropriation and penetration of the Orient, the sense of belatedness produced a peculiarly compulsive will to discover in travelers such as Anne and Wilfrid Blunt and Richard Burton.

The discursive practices of these belated orientalists are therefore split, for they are inscribed within both the economies of colonial power and the exoticist desire for a disappearing Other. Aporia displaces orientalist pseudoscientific certainty here, allowing for the emergence of a schizoid discourse that simultaneously affirms and exposes the ideological discrepancies and political predicaments of colonial hegemony. For the orientalist epistemology to be productive in late colonial relations of power, it had to accommodate an intricate interplay of repetition and innovation, orthodoxy and nonconformity, affirmation and subversion. Orientalist consciousness in the age of colonial dissolution ambivalently interpellates its subjects in a decentered system of opposition and domination, a system that, as Bhabha suggests, can play the role of both supporter and adversary. As I discuss in Chapter 4, even in a bluntly imperialist writer such as Kipling one encounters this split mode of identification. Consider, for example, his inclusion of natives as storytellers in his Anglo-Indian fiction, a narrative technique that brings into focus the colonial writer's mimetic mode of identification and its effects on the production of authority. The symbolic exercise of "white" authorial writing here produces an ambivalent text in which the gesture of exclusion and the return of the excluded complicate the implication of the deflected desire for the Other in colonial relations of power. Kipling's use of "native" voices speaks simultaneously of an appropriative practice—a kind of narcissistic self-acknowledgment that disavows the native's subjectivity—and of a desire for self-exoticism that destabilizes the intentional coded messages of cultural colonialism in Kipling's works. But such effects of splitting, I go on to argue, have a productive function in that they displace blunt modes of racial differentiation and rearticulate them as effects of the growing difference that makes them seem "natural" rather than constructed and imposed.

The kind of discursive ambivalences and ideological uncertainties that one encounters among the belated traveler-writers of the nineteenth century have their genealogical roots in a *desire for the Orient*. In Chapter 1 I define the desire for the Orient, which holds a mediating relation with the orientalist desire for knowledge and power, as a subtle critique of Western superiority and a mode of cultural association with the Other that recognizes the latter's subjectivity. In Nerval's *Voyage en Orient*, the French traveler's relation with the Oriental shifts from distant observation to intimate participation as a result of the return of this repressed desire. The narrator's *désir de l'Orient* displaces the orientalist's egotistic drive for knowledge and compels him to give himself over to everyday experiences of the journey. The desire for the Orient, functioning in mediated opposition to the orientalist's desire for knowledge and mastery, produces the effects of splitting and slippage and prompts a latent practice of decentering both in the case of the speaking subject and in his or her discourse. The belated Orientalism of travelers such as Nerval, Flaubert, Loti, and Eberhardt vacillates between an insatiable search for a counterexperience in the Orient and the melancholic discovery of its impossibility; they are, as a result, discursively diffracted and ideologically split. On the one hand, these texts identify themselves differentially against the encyclopedic *tableau raisonné* and truth claims of official Orientalism by expressing an unease with classification and "objectivity." On the other, they find it impossible to avoid the "baggage" of orientalist knowledge that has mediated the desire to produce an other discourse on the Orient. The representations of these belated travelers thus do not close on an exotic signified but practice an open deferment of signification; they are elliptic discourses, uncertain about their representations and melancholic about their inability to produce an alternative mode of writing about the desired Other.

These discursive ambivalences, however, remain too general to account for the complexities of late Orientalism. The splitting effects of what I have called the desire for the Orient demand further theorization. First, one must describe the conditions of its possibility as a transformational force within the conflicted political field of colonialism. How are we, the postcolonial readers, to locate the functional space of such an elusive force? What are its historical particularities and discursive modalities? What are the critical implications of a desire for the Orient in the political context of the dissymetric relations of colonial encounter? How can it bring about "positive" changes in the relation between Europe and its Other? Second, one must specify the mediated structure of the desire for the Orient in connection with the power that regulates it. What is its potential for strategic utilization by the colonial power? To what extent do the tactics and strategies of domination determine the condition of its possibility? Is the desire for the Other an instance of control by stimulation?

The shift from travelogue to tourist-guide in mid-nineteenth-century orientalist writing provides an instance of discursive slippage where one can locate some of the transformational possibilities of the desire for the Orient that sent masses of European tourists to Eastern countries. Tailored to the needs of amateur travelers in search of leisurely vacations in the

Orient, the discourse of tourism, I suggest in Chapter 2, does not derive its authority from the interpretive power of a centralized subject of enunciation—the meaning-making "I" of the travelogue—but depends for its discursive economy on the possible positions of desire occupied by its readers. As a result, the guide appears to be less an ideological statement about Europe's Other than a dispersed body of practical information about different modes of vacationing in the Orient. The necessary construction of the reading subject as a potential traveler in the tourist discourse, I will argue, problematizes the orientalist desire for knowledge and power and implies a new relation between the European traveler and the Oriental in which the "lordly" practice of signification through fieldwork is displaced by a leisurely tour of exoticism.

And yet, to the extent that the touristic desire for the Orient since the mid-nineteenth century has been embedded in and mediated through the complex and dissymmetric relations of colonial power, the emergence of this new discursive formation and its related practices marks a strategic reconfiguration of European domination. The discourse of tourism unsettles the authority of the Orientalist savant, but it reimplicates its shifting forces in a whole series of new and more efficient relations of power. Not only is the tourist guide itself transformed into a highly sophisticated encyclopedia of orientalist knowledge through an accumulative reproduction of information, but also the tourist industry slowly packages the Orient into a commodity for Western consumption that "homogenizes" the West ideologically as colonialist. Orientalist tourism attests to the productivity of Orientalism and colonialism and their striking ability to utilize the moments of slippage in the process of restructuring their power network.

Orientalism's function in Europe's strategies of domination, I propose in this book, depends on a whole series of discursive and ideological splits that mediate the enabling effects of difference and divergence, effects that can be reappropriated to reinscribe a more effective exercise of power—a "hegemonic" power, if you will—in which everyone is implicated through his or her consent as well as desire. As I will describe more specifically in the case of Anne Blunt's and Eberhardt's travel writings, the belated traveler's solitary quest for elsewhere as a response to the onset of modernity in Europe became crucially productive in the micropolitics of imperial quest during the late nineteenth century. Although both Eberhardt and Blunt adamantly opposed the oppressive practices of late nineteenth-century colonialism, their efforts to produce different and more sympathetic representations of the Orient were appropriated by the

colonial system as valuable information. The copious writings of Eberhardt and Blunt provided French and British colonizers, respectively, with
important data about North African and Bedouin tribes, information that
was then used to subvert their "insurgency." These travelers' discursive
practices confirm that opposition is not necessarily a negative force in
relation to power, but that it can be recuperated as a productive element
in its processes of restructuration and reform. In fact, what allows the
colonial power to sustain its dominant status is its political resilience and
the capacity to utilize effectively its voices of dissent and discontent.

The belatedness of these travelers and their ideological limitations
point to the *relational* character of orientalist formations and the strategies
involved in its productive functioning. Orientalism, I have been suggesting, is not divided into accepted discourses of domination and excluded
discourses of opposition. Rather, such a discourse of power makes al-
lowance for a *circular* system of exchange between stabilizing strategies
and disorienting elements that can produce variant effects. The relations
of orientalist power and knowledge do not constitute a static and unified
structure of distribution. They are organized according to what Foucault
calls a "tactical polyvalence" that maintains an economy of continual variation to suit the shifting needs of its discursive field. Diffused and fluid as
its formation is, Orientalism depends for its economy on the capacity to
bring into contact a plurality of subject and ideological positions. To understand the production of orientalist power and knowledge, therefore,
one must consider the irregular elements beneath the seemingly smooth
surface of its ideological continuity. To ignore the complex interplay of
the disparate practices of Orientalism is to misconceive its complicated
field of power relations.

It is precisely in the context of these discontinuous practices that one
can account for the shifting and transformational nature of orientalist
discourse that *ensures* its cultural hegemony. In a complex field of power
relations such as those of Orientalism and colonialism, the splitting effects
of ambivalent discourses of belated orientalists become catalysts. As odd
points of deflection, they are useful elements in producing a matrix of
transformation in the context of stabilizing forces in the dominant trends
of Orientalism. These belated discourses produce moments of slippage
that inscribe themselves as irreducible opposites in the discursive formation of Orientalism. As such, they establish the necessity of subtle shifts in
the general functioning of its practices and mediate new rules of formation to satisfy the changing conditions of the power relations between
Europe and the Orient.

1. Orientalist Desire, Desire for the Orient: Ideological Splits in Nerval

❖

Desires are already memories.—Italo Calvino, INVISIBLE CITIES

When we speak today of a divided subject, it is never to acknowledge his simple
contradictions, his double postulations, etc.; it is a DIFFRACTION which is intended,
a dispersion of energy in which there remains neither a central core
nor a structure of meaning.—Roland Barthes

The covers of the two-volume Garnier-Flammarion edition of Nerval's
Voyage en Orient are illustrated with two orientalist paintings, Lecomte du
Nouy's *L'Esclave Blanche* and Rosset's *Costumes Orientaux* (see figures 1 and 2).
The first painting depicts a naked Circassian slave woman posing lewdly
with a cigarette in her hand and an intoxicated gaze, representing her idleness in the harem. The second portrays the severity of Oriental veiling,
subtly implying, by the clearly apparent dark eyes of the Oriental woman,
a lasciviousness that must be kept hidden behind the mask. These contrasting images of the Orient are striking, above all, because they point
to the contradictory stereotypes of Oriental life represented so abundantly in European paintings, postcards, and travel writing since the mid-
seventeenth century—stereotypes such as the harem as a site of eroticism,
the Oriental woman as an object for voyeurism, and the veil as a repressive mask. But the paintings are also interesting for the way they represent
the split in the Western vision of its Other: the cleavage of the masked and
the exposed, the "cut" between maximum visibility and total inscruta-
bility, the division between a desire to indulge in corporality and a profound repression of the body.

These paintings and the division of Nerval's text into two volumes seem

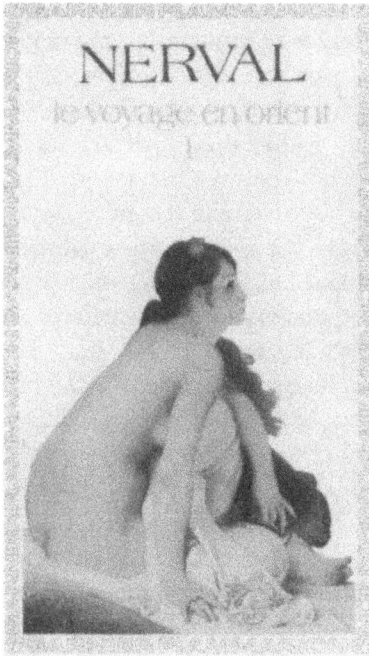

Figures 1 and 2. The cover from Nerval's *Voyage en Orient*, ed. Michel Jeanneret (Paris: Garnier-Flammarion, 1980), vols. 1 and 2. Reproduced by permission of Librairie E. Flammarion.

particularly insightful in the case of a text so split as *Voyage en Orient*. In Nerval, one constantly encounters the opposing poles of orientalist representation: obscurity surrounding the object of representation and an insatiable desire for unveiling inherent in representational practice. The narrative of his journey perpetually vacillates between being a naked representation of the modern Orient and a masked figuration of an orientalist romance, between the blunt generalizations of an "official" orientalist and the more subtle understanding of Oriental culture by an amateur traveler, and between unmasked repetition of the institutional discourses of Orientalism and veiled deflection of them.

The cover paintings can also be taken as an astute comment on Nerval's narrator, whose psychological splits, ideological duplicity, and political division constantly disrupt an already broken discourse. Like the antithetical images of the painted women on the covers, the speaking subject is caught between a fantasy of the Orient as a dream world where his desires are realized and an image of Oriental society as an unattainable, concealed domain of absolute repression. But these paradoxical views of the Orient are not merely textual or subjective contradictions, or even dualities—as most of Nerval's critics have pointed out.[1] Rather, they disclose a historical *split* in the discourse of mid-nineteenth-century Orientalism. I say "split" because, as Roland Barthes points out (see the second epigraph above), it implies dispersion and deflection and is subject to multiplication, whereas "double" indicates a dual and binary relation—Nerval, to use a Barthesian expression, was not contradictory, he was dispersed. My use of the first term, though it has its source in Jacques Lacan's discussion of the subversion of the subject and the splitting phenomenon at the moment of the subject's accession to the symbolic field of social discourses, is not purely psychoanalytical. As I will show later, the split between the speaking subject and her or his discourse has clear political and ideological implications. This splitting, whose dispersing effect eventually subverts the orientalist's certainty, marks the primal division (*Spaltung*, to use Lacan's term)[2] of the subject and his discourse into a conscious (or official) relation to the Orient and a veiled unconscious relation that can manifest itself only in vacillations of the orientalist subject—and only at moments of discursive uncertainty. Masked under the veil of certitude and marginalized by the orientalist's "will to knowledge," the orientalist unconscious—if I may call it that—manifests its disruptive force for the first time in Nerval's *Voyage en Orient*, which, as Edward Said has pointed out in passing, marks a "swerving away from discursive finality of the sort envisioned by previous writers of the Orient."[3]

Mediated Discourse and Split Subjectivity

The comma in the title of this chapter pinpoints the split in the relation of the orientalist subject to the Oriental Other as well as that of the text to the exotic otherness it represents. On the one hand, I am interested in the way Nerval's *Voyage en Orient* repeats and thus participates complicitously in "orientalist desire," that is, the historical urge to "capture" the Other through the official or dominant discourses that the speaking subject has at his or her disposal. Chateaubriand's statement in the preface to the first edition of his *Itinéraire de Paris à Jérusalem* (1811), "I was searching for images; nothing more," provides an appropriate example of the orientalist desire that implies observation and representation without any personal participation in the social reality of the Orient.[4] The experience of the Oriental journey is here viewed either as a kind of scientific research or as a romantic self-discovery; the enunciating subject in both cases assumes the role of a savant in search of (self-)knowledge that must be gained through his or her observations and studies in an "other" place. The Orient, as Constantin de Volney remarks, provides the European with "a field suitable for political and moral observations."[5] The orientalist desire thus involves a conscious act of producing "meaning" for the public from one's personal experience in Oriental countries without any interest in, or recognition of, the Other's subjectivity or culture. On the other hand, I am primarily concerned with the birth of a desire for/of the Orient (*le désir de l'Orient*, to use Nerval's own words) manifested by amateur travelers like Nerval, Eberhardt, or Flaubert whose relations with the Oriental Other included involvement, participation, and indulgence, a kind of giving oneself over to the experience of the Oriental journey without trying to capture the Oriental "signified." Far from being an egoistic drive for knowledge, the desire for the Orient is the return of a repressed fascination with the Other, through whose differentiating function European subjectivity has often defined itself since the Crusades. Beyond their interests in self-realization through their journeys to the Orient, travelers such as Nerval, Eberhardt, and Flaubert had a great desire to understand and even become part of the Oriental culture. Such a desire, as I will discuss shortly, makes the orientalist subject surrender his or her power of representation and pursuit of knowledge by becoming a hedonistic participant in the "immediate" reality of the Oriental culture.[6]

Michel Butor is right to argue that,

> for Nerval, Chateaubriand's journey remains a voyage on the surface [un voyage de surface]. He himself devised his own voyage, utilizing annex centers, lobbies of ellipses encompassing the main points which would allow him, by using parallaxes, to make conspicuous the whole depth of the snare harbored by the normal centers. Roaming through the streets of Cairo, Beirut, and Constantinople, Nerval is always lying in wait for anything that would allow him to sense a cavern extending beneath Rome, Athens, and Jerusalem [cities visited on Chateaubriand's voyage].[7]

At the heart of Nerval's discursive practice is the positivistic belief that a full understanding of the Other is possible through immersion, an extended experience that authorizes the subject to speak about the Oriental.

Unlike his romantic precursor, Nerval always searches beyond the surface
to find what has been ignored by other travelers. Confronting on his
arrival the symbolic veil that blocks his vision, Nerval's narrator begins his
account of the journey with a critique of the superficial traveler:

> But Egypt, solemn and pious, is always the country of enigma and
> mysteries; the beauty surrounds itself, as before, with veils and wrap-
> pings, and this gloomy attitude easily discourages the frivolous Euro-
> pean. He leaves Cairo after eight days and rushes toward the waterfall
> of the Nile, searching for other disappointments which science has in
> store for him, and which will never be suitable to him. For ancient
> initiates, patience was the greatest virtue. Why go so fast? Let us stop
> and attempt to lift a corner of the stern veil of the goddess of Saïs.
> [Mais l'Egypte, grave et pieuse, est toujours le pays des énigmes et des
> mystères; la beauté s'y entoure, comme autrefois, de voiles et de
> bandelettes, et cette morne attitude décourage aisément l'Européen
> frivole. Il abandonne le Caire après huit jours, et se hâte d'aller vers
> les cataractes du Nil chercher d'autres déceptions que lui réserve la
> science, et dont il ne conviendra jamais. La patience était la plus
> grande vertu des initiés antiques. Pourquoi passer si vite? Arrêtons-
> nous, et cherchons à soulever un coin du voile austère de la déesse
> de Saïs.][8]

The traveler here identifies himself differentially: even though Nerval's
narrator considers himself a "touriste" at certain points in his narrative and
feels "deeply unhappy and discouraged" in encountering the practical
difficulties of traveling in Egypt, he is quick to distinguish his philosophy
of the journey from that of his literary precursors, Chateaubriand and
Lamartine. Unlike these early nineteenth-century travelers, who passed
quickly through Cairo and spent most of their time in Haute Egypte in
order to study the historical sites and sacred monuments commonly accepted as archaeologically important, Nerval's narrator is a serious and
patient traveler who wishes to indulge in the enigmatic city and see beyond the obscured appearances, searching for more "authentic" aspects
of its culture. Instead of sliding over the signifiers of otherness in Cairo,
Nerval's narrator is interested in the hidden signifieds of the Oriental city.
The orientalist traveler is also impelled by the epistemophilic desire to
expose what he finds hidden, a desire that in this case is coupled with an
erotic urge to see the imaginary nakedness behind the veil. Nerval's wish
to "soulever un coin du voile austère de la déesse de Saïs" must be read as

both a metaphoric statement about his desire to see beyond the surfaces and a more literal wish to tear the veils of the Oriental women in a voyeuristic attempt to see their hidden bodies.

Ironically, then, the traveler's critique of superficiality—or even scientificity ("d'autres déceptions que lui réserve la science"), depending on how one reads the passage—implicates Nerval's discourse in the orientalist urge to penetrate the Oriental culture. Here the seemingly benevolent desire to see the "real" Orient paradoxically aligns Nerval's discursive practice with that of an earlier precursor, namely Volney. Nerval's praise of patience as the most valuable virtue of a traveler and his interest in the present state of Oriental society echo closely Volney's words: "Most travelers [to the Orient] kept themselves busy with studying the antiquities instead of the modern state; almost all, rushing through the country, have missed two excellent ways to know it: time and the usage of the language."[9] Expressing the orientalist desire to know, Nerval's narrator, like the Cartesian subject, wants to claim an epistemological mastery over the field of his observation, which in turn grants him the authority to represent: "I know/ speak because I was there for a long time." In his "Journal de bord," Nerval's narrator, like the authoritative Volney, even goes so far as to claim access to the voice of truth: "the humble truth does not have the immense resources of dramatic and novelistic devices" (1:337).

Nerval's attempt to go beyond the discursive practice of one set of precursors brings his account of the journey into an affiliation with another precursory mode of representation. In the field of orientalist discourse, the traveler is always inscribed within a filial relationship, and therefore there is no escape from the authority of the *nom-du-père*, the symbolic "Father" who defines the Law of representation. The subject's occasional attempts to overcome the authority of such a dominant figure are precisely what binds him to the Law in a chain of affiliation—denying the authority of Chateaubriand means recognizing Volney's doctrine; and similarly, the rejection of Volney's paternal influence implies the affirmation of Edward William Lane's authorial power; and so on. In short, there is no "outside" to the discourse of Orientalism: to write about the Orient inevitably involves an intertextual relation in which the "new" text necessarily depends for its representational economy on an earlier text. Not only is Nerval's desire for the Orient mediated by the orientalist texts he has read—as I will discuss in more detail shortly—his discursive practice is conditioned by the concepts and strategies of the official or dominant modes of discourse from which his text tries to distinguish itself.

And yet, if Nerval's narrator follows Volney's doctrine of immersion, it is not always to represent the arid "reality" or to frame the Oriental experience in an organized travelogue like his orientalist precursor, but rather to indulge more effectively in the pleasure principle associated with Oriental culture. Nerval, I want to argue, initiated a hedonistic tradition in Orientalism that viewed traveling in the Orient as a leisurely stepping out of the familiar reality of European home, a journey that would ease the cultural ennui associated with daily life—it is not fortuitous that one of the earliest uses of the word *tourist* appears in Nerval, a point to which I will return in Chapter 2. He considered France "the land of coldness and tempests," and he was motivated to travel in the Orient by the desire to spend "some magnificent days amid the Orient's splendid landscapes" (2:363). Thus, in contrast with the journalistic urge to report the events of an explorative journey, in Nerval we encounter a kind of hedonistic spontaneity that turns the occasionally serious orientalist into a man of pleasure, a sort of self-indulgent *flâneur* uninterested in re-producing an already copiously depicted image.[10] As a modern traveler at a time of discursive overproliferation, Nerval's narrator is less interested in engaging in the orientalist activity of "meaning making" than in pursuing an insatiable desire to enter the Orient's image repertoire as a participant—in this sense he can be considered a precursor of modern anthropologists. Having spent a month of nocturnal vagabondage in Constantinople, he wrote, "I did not attempt to represent [peindre] Constantinople; its palaces, mosques, spas, and shores have already been described so many times: I simply wanted to give an idea of a promenade through its streets and squares at the time of major holidays [i.e., Ramadan]" (2:361). Confronted with the excess of discursive production, the traveler abandons his representational practice, recognizing the aesthetics of silence and the pleasure of participation. The power of earlier representations, instead of providing the subject with the authority to represent, discourages him from portraying the Oriental city.

Nerval's account of his journey to Constantinople therefore is not a *representation* but a *figuration*; that is to say, instead of framing what is seen by the subject, the narrative incorporates him into the profile of the very picture it makes, thus eradicating the distant relation of observer and observed object.[11] The month of Ramadan, during which diurnal fasting occasions nocturnal celebration, transforms the exotic into the carnivalesque. Here there is no distinct boundary between an observing subject and an observed Other. Everyone becomes a participant in the nightly spectacle. Nerval's narrator, dressed as a Persian merchant and fully accepted by the tolerant city, spends most of his time in the cafés, indulging in the nocturnal pleasures of the Oriental city. The narrator even claims to have been entertained by "marvelous tales, narrated and declaimed by professional storytellers," a claim that in the case of a traveler who did not speak Arabic suggests a profound desire for self-exoticism, a desire to be an "Other," as he wrote under his photo portrait (2:233).

As a text of pleasure, "Les nuits de Ramazan" recounts the subject's pleasure by reproducing the object of desire—that is, the story itself. The long and suspensefully narrated "Histoire de la Reine du Matin et de Soliman Prince des Génies," though reproduced from its literary sources, splits the representational practice of the orientalist subject, as the narrative of the voyage becomes an imaginary tale divested of most ideological implications of a discourse on the Other. Here there is no claim to "realist" representation, no desire to produce a framed image of a verifiable reality from which nothing emerges but a sign of exoticism. As in the Orient, "everything becomes a tale [tout devient conte]" in which even the reality of the speaking subject is incorporated.

The Orientalist "Baggage"

While the storytellers of Constantinople fill Nerval's narrator with pleasure, the veils of the women of Cairo fill him with frustration and a strong sense of privation. Of course, the orientalist subject has come to Egypt thinking that this is "the land of adventures," an illusion that is shattered by the labyrinthine city and its inaccessible women:

> The night of my arrival in Cairo, I was profoundly sad and discouraged. After riding a few hours on a mule in the company of dragoman, I managed to convince myself that I was going to spend the six most boring months of my life there, and meanwhile everything was organized in advance so that I could not even stay a day less. Is this, I asked myself, the city of *The Thousand and One Nights*, the capital of Fatamite and Sudanese Caliphs? . . . What to expect from this confused labyrinth, perhaps as big as Paris or Rome, from its palaces and its mosques that one counts by the thousand? It seems as if one travels in a dream in a bygone city, inhabited solely by ghosts who people it without animating it. Each neighborhood, surrounded by crenellated walls and closed in by heavy doors as in the Middle Ages, still retains the physiognomy that it probably had during the time of Saladin. (1:151)

This passage embodies the orientalist stereotype of the Orient as an inevitably fixed but decaying region. But Nerval's claim about the discrepancy between the reality of the Orient and its fantastic image repertoire in *The Thousand and One Nights* points to the mimetic nature of the desire for the Orient. The folkloric tales of *The Thousand and One Nights* constitute an orientalist imaginary in which the possibility of an elsewhere seems real. But the orientalist subject's encounter with the "real" can only be an experience of discontentment because his vision is mediated by the symbolic field of cultural "baggage" that has given him the illusion of a phantasmagoric city. The fantastic tales of *The Thousand and One Nights*, which the orientalist has been made to see as a "true" representation of Oriental reality, comes between the narrator and the immediate reality, exposing the mimetic nature of his desire. The intertext constantly haunts the subject's imagination as he travels through the Orient. Nerval's narrator repeatedly acknowledges it: "Since my arrival in Cairo, all the tales of *The Thousand and One Nights* pass through my head, and I see in my dreams all the demons and giants unleashed since Salamon" (1:164). The experience of the orientalist subject therefore can be meaningful only in relation to the intertextual context of the discursive domain in which he participates.[12] As Michel Jeanneret so cogently puts it, "in Nerval, experience is perceived—or in any case, recounted—through remembered readings [souvenirs de lecture]. A curtain of erudition and bookish models [modèles livresques] come between the subject and the world, so that it is often impossible to decide what the status of the referent is: lived or read? immediate or textual?"[13] The orientalist representation is thus always a re-presentation of the Orient: The narrative of the voyage is not, and perhaps, one should add, cannot be, a direct transcription of the reality seen by the enunciating subject; it is either a rewriting of the precursor's text—from which he derives his authority—or the reexperience of a phantasmatic text. The subject's inauguration into the field of desire always passes through the "defiles" of signifiers that are purely textual. As a result, the subject's desire for the Orient is not the desire for the Other; rather, it is a desire defined for him by the orientalist intertext. Or, to put it slightly differently, the desire for the Orient is necessarily mediated through the orientalist's desire itself, and thus the intertext always implicates the traveler in the field of orientalist power relations.

Moreover, the fantastic stories of the mediating text, ironically, make the "real" experience of the city appear like a dream in which everything is thrown into an oblique past. In the world of such mediated vision,

Cairo thus loses its *presence* and becomes a "fallen capital," a "vast grave," just as its inhabitants seem to be ghosts. The representational forces of the intertext go beyond the power of the traveler's own vision; Nerval's narrator is engulfed by the referential illusion that problematizes his direct relation with "immediate" reality. The discursive power of orientalist intertexts always furnishes the orientalist subject with an earlier vision of the Orient. Throughout his stay in Cairo, Nerval's traveler constantly questions the reality of the "real": "Was that a part of a dream or of life?" (1:152). As the boundaries of the real and the imaginary blur, the subject's dreams, perceived through his earlier readings, eventually gain the status of the real. In the wake of his departure, Nerval's schizoid narrator paradoxically reaffirms the accuracy of his mediated vision:

> I leave regretfully this old city of Cairo where I found the last traces of the Arab spirit [du génie arabe], and which did not betray the ideas that I had formed about it from the tales and traditions of the Orient. I had seen it so many times in childhood dreams that it seemed to me as if I had stayed there, but I don't know when; I reconstructed my ancient Cairo in the middle of deserted districts and crumbling mosques! It seemed as if I was retracing my old steps [j'imprimais les pieds dans la trace de mes pas anciens]; . . . I told myself, in going around this wall, in passing this door, I would see a certain thing . . . and the thing was there, ruined, but real. (1:296)

These remarks are interesting, above all, as a testimony to the symbolic power of the orientalist intertext that has construed the Oriental journey as a childhood fantasy. The traveler's experience is consequently a revision of what he had already seen in his dreams. The passage betrays the ideological splits in such a mediated vision. To be sure, the subject of enunciation is clearly alienated with respect to his own representation, since the weight of the official discourse of Orientalism forces him to affirm the authority that he has inherited from the precursor without considering the implications of such a reaffirmation for the narrative economy. Read against the narrator's reflections just after his arrival in Cairo, this passage brings to the surface the consequences of the splits in the subject and his discourse: the phantoms now become the last survivors of the Arab spirit; *The Thousand and One Nights* turns out to be a dependable source of information about the Orient; and the uncanny labyrinthine corridors of Cairo are, after all, the familiar images visited in childhood dreams. Just as the subject thinks that he is walking on the traces of his old tracks, Nerval's narrative ruminates on the traces of earlier textual representations. These reversals are not so much contradictory, given the split nature of narrative economy, as affirmative in that they validate the perception of the mediating intertext while simultaneously confirming the traveler's earlier impression: Cairo is *still* a deposed capital where "everywhere stone crumbles and wood rots" (1:151); the narrator *still* feels like he is traveling in a dream; and the subject's experience is *still* one of disappointment and depression. Counterintuitive though it may seem, splits actually produce a sense of consistency in Nerval's discourse, for they normalize what the text posits as difference. I will later return to the productive function of split identity in Nerval, but for the moment I want to address the implications of the traveler's mediated vision.

The mediating function of the intertext that comes between the traveler and the Other provides the conditions of desire. First, the subject's desire for the Orient is stimulated by the city's inaccessibility, which blocks his vision—repression here has a productive function. It is for this reason that the narrator tells the reader he intends to stay in Cairo for a while in order to "lift a corner of the stern veil of the goddess of Saïs." The Oriental veil does not annul the subject's desire; rather, it arouses his scopic urge to overcome the barrier. As the traveler himself admits, "Imagination benefits from this incognito of feminine faces which does not extend to all their charms [L'imagination trouve son compte à cet incognito des visages féminins, qui ne s'étend pas à tous leurs charmes]" (1:150). For the object of desire to be discovered by the subject, it must be absent—or at least initially inaccessible.[14] The veil of the Oriental woman conveys a kind of lack, the absence or concealment of the object that arouses his desire for unity with the Other; as Lacan has shown, desire is a *défense*, meaning both "defense" and "prohibition."[15] For the Western viewer the veil signifies a prohibition that governs his desire by providing a limit to his *jouissance*. The mask also eroticizes what is seen by the subject: "Beautiful hands ornamented with talismanic rings and silver bracelets, sometimes pale marble arms completely escaping the large sleeves rolled up underneath the shoulder, bare feet loaded with rings that the *babouch* [oriental slipper] abandons at each step, and which reverberate around the ankles with a silvery noise [les chevilles résonnent d'un bruit argentin]: here is what is permissible to admire, to guess, to surprise, to discover without the crowd getting nervous about it or the woman herself seeming to notice" (1:150). The concealment of the body multiplies the signifiers of desire. Everything, from the hands of the veiled women to the pieces of jewelry that ornament her body, becomes a partial object, a metonymy of desire which perpetuates the subject's attempt to fill the gap in the chain of signifiers of his desire as he satisfies his voyeuristic urge—an urge that is itself only a metaphoric substitution for his insatiable desire. Such desire, then, is a kind of *méconnaissance*, a negatively constructed identification, as concealment becomes the cause and condition of desirability.

Second, the fullness of the signifiers of the intertext—initially defining the Other as the field of desire and fantasy—exposes the emptiness of the signifieds in the subject's encounter with the real. Whereas in the intertext the Orient appears to *possess* the desired object, in reality the Oriental Other appears to lack the object of desire. The narrator's melancholic reflections on his arrival and departure, quoted above, pinpoint the discovery of the lack, the Orient as emptied space: Egypt is "the land of dreams and illusion," and the phantasmic Cairo "live[s] under ash and dust" (1:151, 296). The subject's desire for the Orient begins to take shape in the gap between the "reality" of the Orient emerging before him from dust and dream and the phantasm of the Orient conveyed to him through the symbolic field of the orientalist intertext.

The experience of this ontological break (*écart*) is what makes the subject recognize the identity of his desire as a lack, as an absence: "In Africa, one dreams about India, just as in Europe one dreams about Africa: the ideal always radiates beyond our actual horizon" (1:262). Desire always lies where the subject is *not*, in a beyond that, once achieved, points to another beyond in a chain of signifiers that can end only in death. For this reason, the desired Orient is essentially identified as death by the subject. The narrator's first impression, that "Egypt is a vast grave," and his last observation, that "this cult of death is an eternal feature of Egyptian nature; at least it serves to protect and pass on to the world the dazzling history of its past"—beyond the conscious repetition of an orientalist stereotype—disclose an unconscious recognition of death as that in which the chain of signifiers of the desire of the Orient are anchored (1:146, 296). It is death that protects and transmits the subject's journey through the "defiles" of signifiers, and it is precisely this primordial absence that motivates the subject's quest for Oriental paradise, the search for a beyond that always lies somewhere *he is not*.

Orientalist Authority and Its Discontents

In the field of such a politically charged discourse as Orientalism, the psychological splits in the traveler and the narrative uncertainties in the text he or she produces—which I have been discussing up to this point—

bear clear political implications, to which I turn by way of conclusion. Here, too, there are divisions and vacillations, affirmative signs and interventionary gestures, departing moves and returning tendencies, constructive attempts and disruptive shifts. In *Voyage en Orient*, authority is not produced through strategies of disavowal, nor does it have a repressive function. Rather, it is the effect of a splitting difference enacted on both subjective and narrative levels. The traveler's desire for the Orient, which I have described as a mimetic and therefore mediated phenomenon, is productive of difference, of diffraction in the relation between the orientalist and the Other. The desire for the Orient is a hybrid force that posits uncertainty in the orientalist's consciousness and enables possibilities of dialogic articulation because it propagates different identity effects and ideological positions. Edward Said argues that "every interpretation, every structure created for the Orient, . . . is a reinterpretation, a rebuilding of it."[16] But Nerval's *Voyage en Orient* demonstrates that repetition always produces difference, that restructuring comes with diffracting and differentiating effects, effects that can be critical of orientalist assumptions. Consider, for example, how on a purely thematic and conscious level the discrepancy between the phantasmic images of the Other inherited from the orientalist tradition and the traveler's personal experience in the Orient leads Nerval to question the conventional European views of Oriental culture—I mean here the identification of the Orient as "*le pays d'aventures*," a domain of lustful sensuality and an absolutely lawless region where "everything . . . is possible." Having (supposedly) visited the harem of the viceroy in Egypt, Nerval writes: "Here is another illusion that one must lose: the delights of the harem [*délices du harem*], the omnipotence of the husband or the master, the charming women united to make only one person happy [i.e., the sultan]. The religion or customs temper in a peculiar way this ideal that has seduced so many Europeans. All of those who, on the strength of our prejudices, had thus understood Oriental life, found themselves discouraged in a very short time" (1:268).[17] The traveler is here divided into a critic of the traditional perception of Oriental culture and a nostalgic supporter of that myth. His description of the harem as a "delightful" illusion and "ideal" fantasy, on the one hand, suggests his reluctance to abandon the myth. Nerval's narrator seems, in fact, quite nostalgic about the time when, ignorant of the reality, the harem was a seductive fantasy. Yet, on the other hand, his nostalgia here enables the possibility of demystifying the European myth of the harem. His reference to European prejudices suggests a dialogic consciousness that deflects the authority of orientalist discourse as the traveler's nostalgic desire for the romance of the harem produces a critical attitude toward orientalist myths that have led him to believe such an illusion.

Nerval's narrator takes a step even further from his project of demystification as he engages the problem of cultural differences, which he considers the source of European misconstruction of Oriental sexuality: "Their beliefs and their customs differ so much from ours that we can only judge them from the perspective of our own relative depravity. If one understood the dignity and the very chastity of the relations that exist between a Muslim man and his wives, one would renounce the whole voluptuous mirage that was created by our eighteenth-century writers" (2:358). This statement more closely resembles a passage from a text like Abdelwahab Bouhdiba's *La sexualité en Islam* than an orientalist *récit de voyage*. Not only does the narrator reject the "voluptuous mirage" of eighteenth-century Orientalism, he also calls into question the European essentialist tendency to judge the Other according to European norms and values. Even more subversive is the subtle, perhaps even unconscious, connection he makes between the two, claiming that the European fantasy of Oriental sexuality is a projection of Europe's own depravity and prejudice: in the first passage "our prejudices," and in the second "our own relative depravity" are viewed as the cause of the misconstruction of sexual relations in the Orient. The narrator seems to realize that though the eroticization of the Orient had its genesis in eighteenth-century romances, what perpetuated it throughout the nineteenth century was the power of interpretation and judgment Europeans had at their disposal. The narrator's recognition of the unbridgeable cultural differences problematizes any dichotomy of self/other in which the first term would be invariably privileged and empowered.

And yet, to the extent to which these thematic and conscious gestures of subversion are only one aspect of the multifaceted ideology of a text such as *Voyage en Orient*, they are not in themselves politically decisive, for they are thematically contradicted by other, ideologically affirmative, aspects of the split text. The subversive gestures do become ideologically significant, however, if they are read precisely as a splitting force that prompts an unconscious practice of decentering both in the case of the enunciating subject and in his discursive practice. What most sharply differentiates *Voyage en Orient*—and its speaking subject, of course—from earlier orientalist travelogues is the way that it puts into practice a complex interplay of thematically and ideologically heterogeneous positions which disrupt the narrative unity and discursive order that are characteristic of the official and scientific discourses of Orientalism. The opposing poles of Nerval's ambivalent text challenge the certitude of the authoritative orientalist subject and his or her assertive discourse.

The narrator's final remarks bring into focus Nerval's discontinuous mode of representation:

> What more will I tell you, my friend? What would be of interest to you in these jerky and diffused letters, mingled with fragments of travel journal and legends collected by chance? This very disorder is the guarantee of my sincerity; what I wrote I have seen and felt—was I wrong to report so naively thousands of minute incidents, disdained ordinarily in the picturesque or scientific voyages?
>
> Do I have to defend myself to you for my continual admiration of diverse religions of the countries I have crossed? Yes, I felt pagan in Greece, Muslim in Egypt, pantheist among the Druzes, and devoted on the seas of heavenly stars of Chaldea. (2:363)

These interrogative sentences can be read, on one level, as rhetorical questions in support of the indicative claim of the conscious subject that what he has reported is a truthful representation of what he saw in the Orient. The framing of the only indicative sentence by the interrogative sentences in the first paragraph points to the centrality of the authorial "will to truth" that he inherited from Volney. The narrator here posits himself as the "objective" subject of enunciation, producing a "truthful" representation of the Orient based on what he saw there. The traveler's insistence on experience also imparts authority to his discourse, making his representation seem a "truthful" account of the Oriental culture. In this sense, the final remarks are affirmative and consistent with the dominant ideologies of orientalist discourse.

But the narrator's final words can also be interpreted, on another level, as real questions, unconsciously unmasking the uncertainty surrounding the split text and its divided narrator, for *Voyage en Orient* is a jumbled, diffuse, and fragmentary text, and its enunciating subject is also plural and dispersed: Nerval's account of his journey invokes conventional expectations of a phantasmagoric Orient while simultaneously displaying their fictionality; his discursive practice imitates the pseudoscientific style of Volney while ironizing its sobriety; and Nerval's narrator reaffirms the authority of his orientalist precursors while at the same time problematizing it by exposing the shortcomings of their vision.

Nerval's *Voyage en Orient*, I suggest, forms the threshold of a split Orientalism in which the desire for the Orient forces the repressed contradictions
and tensions in the dominant ideology of the official Orientalism to return, symptomatically, in a disruptive fashion. The belated traveler's desire
for the "authentic" Orient and his discovery of its absence engendered a
new kind of orientalist praxis, one marked by ambivalence and uncertainty. More important, Nerval's narrative, as the site of an ideological
diffraction, engages the fundamental issue of the European savant having
moral and political responsibility over the Other and implicitly problematizes his power of representation. In Nerval we encounter—perhaps for
the first time—the appearance of a self-questioning mode of representation in which the boundaries of the imaginary and the real blur, and the
distinctions between the phantasmic vision of the Other and the scientific
and institutional approaches to the Orient have collapsed. Nerval's *Voyage
en Orient* is, in short, the site of a discursive drift constantly fluctuating
between an orientalist urge to represent "objectively" the Other and the
disquieting recognition of the representation's fallacies.

What is at stake in Nerval's text is not just the narrator's *"conscience de soi,"*
as Michel Jeanneret has argued, but the identity of a politically more
significant figure, the orientalist. True, everyone in nineteenth-century
France was an orientalist, as Victor Hugo points out in his preface to *Les
Orientales*. But the disharmonizing effect of Nerval's discursive practice and
the readily apparent problem of split identity in the *sujet d'énonciation*, as
effects of the desire for the Orient, nonetheless produce a fracture, an
"odd" moment in the orientalist discourse and in the position of its
practitioners. Given that Orientalism, like any other discourse,[18] is con-
trolled and organized by certain procedures that create a sense of order
and unity, repressing its ambivalences and contradictions under a mask of
sobriety and confidence, Nerval's *Voyage en Orient* is potentially disruptive
in that it unveils the ideological splits in orientalist discourse and articulates the discontinuities in its epistemological status. The irregularities of
Nerval's narrative, the splits in its speaking subject, and the uncertainty
surrounding its discourse are, to use Foucault's words, "fracturing units,"
or subtle ruptures in Orientalism's discursive system, and tactical shifts
away from its ideologically dominant mode of representation.

But to say that there is a deviation from the official mode of orientalist
discourse in Nerval is not to claim that such a text is "exterior" to Orientalism. In a dominant discursive practice such as Orientalism there is no
radical rupture or pure ideological resistance; indeed, writing about the

Orient unavoidably implies entering the strategic field of its power relations. But neither does the ubiquity of Orientalism mean that deviation from its dominant strategies of representation is impossible, or that it is a lure betraying the idealist subject in search of counterculture. Rather, Orientalism depends for its authority on the productive effects of splitting discourses such as Nerval's, for, as Homi Bhabha argues, hybridity is the sign of productivity of dominant discourses. The desire for the Orient in Nerval, for example, deflects the orientalist desire for knowledge and power and introduces certain modes of change in representing the Oriental Other. But these changes are produced by Orientalism as part of its discursive system and are therefore reimplicated in its dominant strategies of representation. The shifts and deflections in split texts such as *Voyage en Orient* catalyze changes in the dominant orientalist discourses that mediate them, and as such contribute to the much-needed process of discursive restructuring. These split discourses, as I will demonstrate in Chapter 6, are the "noise" of Orientalism's communication system. They create a temporary effect of disorder that eventually helps to transform Orientalism's strategies of domination, for they expose the system's shortcomings. The process of restructuration in Orientalism works through the disorienting effects of hybrid identities and ambivalent discourses.

2. From Travelogue to Tourist Guide: The Orientalist as Sightseer

✺

Nerval's melancholy reflections at the very beginning of his *Voyage en Orient* are an early instance of the discursive shift in orientalist travel literature from travelogue to tourist guidebook:

> I don't know if you will be interested in peregrinations of a tourist leaving Paris in full November. This is a fairly sad litany of misadventures [une assez triste litanie de mésaventures]; it is a rather weak description to offer, a painting without horizon, without scenery where it becomes impossible to utilize the three or four views of Switzerland or Italy that were done before leaving, the melancholic reveries on the sea, the vague poetry of the lakes, the alpine *études* and all the poetic flora of warmer climes that give the Parisian bourgeois so much bitter regret for not being able to go any farther than Montreuil or Montmorency. (1:55)

Nerval's nostalgia for a time when "real" adventures in unknown lands were possible and his derogatory use of the word *touriste*—which appeared in the French language only in 1816—can be taken as signals of a genealogical discontinuity in the identity of the orientalist. They announce the gradual disappearance of the adventurous traveler who undertook the troublesome journey in search of new "knowledge," romantic encounters, and exotic experiences.[1]

The development of steamships revolutionized travel on the Mediterranean, and the construction of railroad lines between Oriental cities by European colonizers—such as the Alexandria-Cairo and Cairo-Assouan lines in Egypt and the Symern-Aydin and Constantinople lines in Asia Minor—furnished western European travelers with the comfort indispensable in encouraging them to make the long journey across the Orient. Moreover, the French occupation of Maghreb, the British presence in India and Egypt and their use of Alexandria as a transfer station to India, and the ending of the Greco-Turkish conflicts in 1828 "stabilized" the sociopolitical situation in the Orient, providing the necessary security for the tourist industry. Although the ordinary Parisian bourgeois could not afford to go beyond Montreuil and Montmorency—great tourist resorts during the mid-nineteenth century in France—the improved traveling conditions made the Oriental journey, once an arduous, demanding, and ambitious endeavor, an easier, less time-consuming, and more practical and efficient enterprise, and thus generated a steady flow of western European tourism to the Orient. If at one time travelers like Volney and Chateaubriand had to spend a fortune—Volney, for example, spent almost his whole inheritance to finance his Oriental journey—the new facilities permitted more of the ordinary sort of travelers to go. Flaubert's trip to Alexandria, for example, took eight days, compared with an already shortened voyage of fifteen days by Nerval five years earlier.[2]

Nerval's preliminary reflections in *Voyage en Orient* are also illuminating as a critical reference to a "new" discursive formation, namely, the tourist guide.[3] Like Roland Barthes's description of the *Guide Bleu* in *Mythologies*, Nerval's text characterizes the new genre as a "poor" representation devoid of aesthetic consciousness, a prosaic picture without the poetic horizon of the earlier travelogues, and a vague narrative that lacks the heroic adventures of a romantic traveler and is unable to properly depict his gloomy musing on the sea and the poetic flora of the Orient. Nerval's uncertainty as to whether his itinerary would be of interest to readers points to the prevalent stereotypical view of the tourist guide as an uninteresting, superficial (if not vulgar) representation in the service of the lazy bourgeois, who, as Barthes argues, savors "a newborn euphoria in buying effort, in keeping its image and virtue without feeling any of its malaise."[4]

Although such characterizations of the tourist and the guide that leads him or her through the journey are partly accurate in that the tourist is more passive and less engaged in heroic adventure, and the tourist guide is a product of bourgeois consumerism, they seem genealogically problematic, for they disregard the historical situation that brought about their existence. Contrary to Barthes's claim that the tourist guide "testifies to the futility of all analytical descriptions, those which reject both explanations and phenomenology," the "informational" nature of the guide is actually a significant shift in travel literature which serves the current needs of the power structure that supports it (75).[5] My intention here is not, however, to make an apology for the tourist guide or the tourist, as Dean MacCannell, Jonathan Culler, and others have done.[6] Indeed, I will argue in this chapter that while the discourse of tourism problematizes the authority of the orientalist, it reimplicates that authority in a new and more complex set of power relations between the European tourist and the Orient. In this sense, my reading of the mid-nineteenth-century guides in France and England is affiliated with such social critics as Susan Buck-Morss, Dennison Nash, and others who argue that tourism (in the "Third World") is "an extension of cultural domination" by the industrial nations.[7] More specifically, however, my aim in this chapter is to map the discursive formation of the tourist guide as the prevalent mode of discourse in orientalist travel literature during the mid-nineteenth century in France and England. While reading two of the earliest tourist guides, Quetin's *Guide en Orient* and John Murray's *Hand-Book for Travellers in the Ionian Islands, Greece, Turkey, Asia Minor, and Constantinople* as examples of the early orientalist tourist guide, I will address two sets of questions. First, how did the tourist guide as a new discursive formation define itself against its precursory genre, the travelogue? How can one describe its discursive field and the correlations between its statements? Or, what rules governed its formation in the historical context of the other discourses of mid-nineteenth-century Orientalism? Second, what are the political and historical implications of such a discursive shift? How does this discursive shift correspond historically to the changes and needs of the power structure that supported it and benefited from it? Is the ideological status of such a discourse "oppositional" or "affirmative" in relation to the general context of Orientalism and its field of power relations?

Discursive Formation: A Theoretical Qualification

To say that a new discursive formation such as the tourist guide replaced the travelogue does not necessarily suggest that the travelogue completely disappeared. Nor does it mean that all of a sudden a new discourse appeared, replacing all the discursive regularities and "enunciative modalities" of the travelogue.[8] To define a new discursive formation necessarily implies a return to and a repetition of the previous discursive formation. Michel Foucault explains this in *The Archaeology of Knowledge:*

To say that one discursive formation is substituted for another is not to say that a whole world of absolutely new objects, enunciations, concepts, and theoretical choices emerges fully armed and fully organized in text that will place that world once and for all; it is to say that a general transformation of relations has occurred, but that it does not necessarily alter all the elements; it is to say that statements are governed by new rules of formation, it is not to say that all objects or concepts, all enunciations or all theoretical choices disappear. On the contrary, one can, on the basis of these new rules, describe and analyse phenomena of continuity, return, and repetition. (173)

The shift from the travelogue to the tourist guide must be viewed not just as a transformational change in the representational practice of Orientalism but also as a discursive repetition. It is precisely these constant modes of separation and return that allow the possibility of multiplication and the dispersion of statements; and these in turn reinforce Orientalism as the official discourse invested with the power of representing Europe's Other, for as I argue in the Introduction, Orientalism depends on a principle of discontinuity for its authority. Although in the process of delineating its formation—the types of its statements, the rules of their divisions and regroupings, and so on—the tourist guide distinguishes itself from the travelogue and suggests a general transformation of discursive practices; it is in a relation of coexistence with the precursory discourse in reproducing similar elements and concepts. The large body of knowledge borrowed from orientalist travelogues provides a "field of presence"—that is, statements borrowed from another field of knowledge in a given discourse—for the tourist book: the guide quotes the statements of previous travelers, incorporates them as part of its informational apparatus, and then acknowledges them as truthful representations of the Orient. Quetin's *Guide en Orient*, for example, begins its chapter on Egypt with a long quotation from Volney's *Les Ruines*, followed by a long description of "marvelous Egypt" that includes images taken from religious and historical observations of other travelers such as Chateaubriand and Lamartine. Similarly, Murray's *Hand-Book* includes quotations from Thomas Hope's *Anastasius*, Sir Charles Fellows's *Travels and Researches in Asia Minor*, Joseph F. von Hammer-Purgstall's reflections on Constantinople, and Lord Byron's orientalist poetry. The tourist is thus constantly encouraged to experience the Orient through the mediation of earlier orientalist narratives: the view of the harbor of Ephesus justifies Byron's romantic description of it, Syria brings to mind Lamartine's religious reflections in the Levant, the Oriental traveling merchant reminds the tourist of such figures in Genesis, and so on.

Enunciative Modalities of the Guide

Orientalist tourist guides appeared almost simultaneously in France and England during the mid-nineteenth century. In France, as Jean-Claude Berchet indicates, Marchebeus's *Voyage de Paris à Constantinople par bateau à vapeur; nouvel itinéraire orné de 50 vues et vignettes sur acier* . . . (1839) was the first. It was soon replaced by Quetin's more practical *Guide en Orient* in 1846, followed in 1861 by a series of guides published by Joanne. In England, London publisher John Murray's *Hand-Book for Travellers in the Ionian Islands, Greece, Turkey, Asia Minor, and Constantinople* (1840) and later the *Hand-Book for Travellers in India and Pakistan, Burma and Ceylon* (1859) gave him a monopoly on tourist guide production. These guides belonged to the same discursive category and held a similar epistemological status as the Blue Books, the British government reports on domestic social conditions. They were, in other words, systematic bodies of encyclopedic knowledge that provided the traveler with information on everything from how to prepare for such an important journey to detailed descriptions of roads, historical monuments, religions, languages, racial categories, and government structures in Oriental countries.

As a result, the tourist guide as a modern orientalist discourse is a dispersed, heterogeneous text, belonging at once to several different epistemological domains in its representation of the Orient: historical knowledge is provided to situate the Orient in its irretrievable past, while geographical data mark it spatially; ethnographic notes and reports characterize the Orientals, and architectural details describe their living environment; general philosophical reflections at the outset prepare the tourist ideologically, while monetary and commercial information provide him or her with a "business report." These guides were not only designed for travelers in the Orient, they were also read by people who had no immediate plans for an Oriental journey but read them like travelogues to satisfy their desire for knowledge about exotic lands and their racially Other inhabitants.[9]

Yet, what most sharply differentiates these tourist guides as a discourse "representing" the Orient from travelogues that had a similar discursive function is the situation of the speaking subject. The travelogue is a discourse dependent for its textual economy on certain enunciative modalities from which it borrows its authority. The travelogue often, if not always, begins with prefatory remarks that raise and address the general questions of who speaks, in the name of what, and for which particular reasons. Richard Burton's preliminary "words concerning what induced [him] to a pilgrimage" to El Medinah and Meccah are an appropriate example of the formation of enunciative modalities in the discourse of the travelogue: he introduces himself as a "doughty" soldier-traveler in the service of the Royal Geographical Society of London "for the purpose of removing that opprobrium of modern adventure, the huge white blot which in our maps still notes the eastern and the central regions of Arabia."[10] Not only does Burton introduce his institutional affiliation, which legitimates his discourse, he also delineates the specific purpose of his travel, which in the context of his institutional relation provides him with the authority to recount his journey. A similar discursive justification and legitimization mark the beginning of Volney's *Voyage en Syrie et en Egypte* where he presents himself as a savant making certain "observations politiques et morales" in the Orient to satisfy his own and his readers' *passion* for knowledge about the Orientals while at the same time contributing to the epistemological field of Oriental studies.[11]

The tourist guide, on the contrary, is a discourse in which the statements and their speakers are dissociated from one another, thus allowing the dispersion of the enunciative function. Instead of the "author," it is usually the publisher—John Murray, for example—who takes responsibility for the production of the guide. Even when the name of the editor as the collector of information is mentioned, it is qualified by statements dissociating him from the totality of the text. In the preface to the sixteenth edition of Murray's *Hand-Book for Travellers in India and Pakistan, Burma and Ceylon* (1949), the publisher lists the various revisions and reprints, the names of the different editors of earlier editions, the subtle regroupings of the materials in the process of revising the guide, the reconstructions of the directory and the index, and the additional information that had been added to Captain E. M. Eastwick's first edition, thus denying any central voice in its discourse. Interestingly, the publisher even solicits the help of the tourist, requesting that "errors and omissions may be communicated to Mr. Murray, on a postcard if desired" (vii). The publisher then acknowledges the "voluntary co-operation and courteous assistance freely offered" by the Indian government and British officers in the field. Unlike the unifying function of the first-person narrator in the travelogue, the enunciative modalities here imply the dispersion of the speaking subject. The discourse of tourism is no longer the expression of a centralized, consistent, and unique subject of enunciation whose prefatory identification defines the autobiographical mode of his discursive production; rather, the tourist guide frames its information through the dispersion of a plurality of voices and the exposure of their discontinuities.

The disappearance of the author as an acknowledged orientalist in the tourist guide means, of course, the emergence—and the recognition—of the reader-user as an orientalist. The travelogue produces its first-person subject ("I") as the site of an act of interpretation—"making sense" of the Orient—and as someone who is authorized to *make* meaning. The centrality and discursive authority of the first-person subject in turn imply exclusion, separating the orientalist and his or her experience from the reader, whose desire for exoticism can be satisfied only as a displacement of or identification with the enunciative subject's desire, realized in his Oriental journey. Such a differential positioning is often delineated in the very beginning of the travelogue where the traveler describes the difficult conditions of the journey and the egotistical satisfaction in pursuing such an arduous journey—Burton, for instance, makes "no apology for the egotistical semblance of [his] narrative" (21)—and the ways his account of the itinerary can be pedagogically beneficial to the reader. The tourist guide, on the other hand, constructs the reading subject ("you") as a *potential traveler* and presupposes the realization of its addressee's desire for the Orient. Quetin's *Guide en Orient*, for instance, begins with such a recognition as it describes the different itineraries of its implied users based on their hypothetical needs, ranging from a complete tour of the Orient, including every country from Greece to Turkey, to a hurried trip to Constantinople. In contrast to the exclusionary style of the travelogue, one encounters in the discourse of tourism an obsessive desire to include, to incorporate every kind of traveler in its applied domain. Quetin's *Guide du voyageur en Algérie* (1846), for example, mentions various types of traveler in its subtitle, such as *le savant, l'artiste, l'homme du monde* [the worldly man], and even *le colon* [the colonial settler]. These categories suggest different domains of intervention in the Orient to which the guide's information applies. I will return later in this chapter to these guides' fields of application, especially in the context of colonial interests, but for the moment I want to address the productive relation between the guide's inclusive tendency and tourist desire.

There is even a conscious attempt to augment the reader's desire for exoticism and tempt him or her to make the journey by promising satisfaction. Quetin's guide describes "the Orient" as a "theatre of so many great events," a "land of marvels" where "the peregrination of the traveler is of most interest" (1). A more elaborated version of such "travel agent" blurbs is offered at the beginning of Murray's Hand-Book for Travelers in the Ionian Islands, Greece, Turkey and Constantinople:

> You are in immediate contact with nature. Every circumstance of scenery and climate becomes of interest and value, and the minutest incident of country, or of local habits cannot escape observation. A burning sun may sometime exhaust, or a summer-storm may drench you, but what can be more exhilarating than the sight of the length-ened troop of variegated and gay costumes dashing at the full speed along to the crack of the Tartar whip and the wild whoop of the surugee? . . . You are constantly in the full enjoyment of the open air of a heavenly climate,—its lightness passes to the spirits,—its serenity sinks into the mind. (i–ii)

The very use of the present tense is indicative of the way the guidebook claims the realization of its reader's fantasy as an immediate and possible reality—in contrast with the retrospective discourse of the travelogue, which implies a geographical distance between the reading position and the visited Orient. As in Quetin's guide, the Orient is again represented as a "natural" theater where the tourist can observe exotically untouched scenery, the local habits and costumes, and the exhilarating show of colorful Tartar troops. The description of the Oriental landscape, ironically, functions as a set of stage directions for the imaginative enactment by the reader of the scene it describes—here the domains of textuality and traveling merge. In the first sentence—"You are in immediate contact with nature"—the would-be tourist is directed by the mediation of the guide to reproduce, to rehearse (répéter) in his or her mind's eye the exotic original. The tourist guide is thus a discursive formation that defines its authority in a mediating relation to the reader's desire for exoticism—the desire that in orientalist travelogues was more the attribute of the narrative subject. Here the Oriental journey is represented not as the "experimentum crucis" of a privileged subject, to use Burton's terms, but as a recreational, leisurely tour of exoticism available to a wide range of readers and chock-full of pleasure, exhilarating experiences, and picturesque encounters—encounters to be produced by the tourist, not simply described by a narrator. I will return later to the political implications of the arousal of such a belated desire for exoticism in the context of the tourist industry, but for the moment suffice it to say that such a desire is not exterior to the discourse of tourism. Rather, the latter is a "formative" element in the discursive formation of the tourist guide, which has to represent itself as an instrument for the realization of the tourist's desire for exoticism, a desire that, as I suggest in the Introduction, is fraught with an anxiety of belatedness in relation to such adventures. The tourist guide, in short, depends for its authority on including within its own discursive practice an exhaustive enumeration of possible positions of the reader's desire that would eventually be reimplicated in European colonialism abroad.[12]

From Narration to Description: Grids of Specification

The dispersive nature of enunciative modalities in the tourist guide implies a shift from narration to description as the dominant mode of orientalist representation. What differentiates the representational mode of the guide from that of the travelogue is the nonlinearity of its statements, which are neither arranged around the presence of an author nor recorded as a direct account of an earlier journey. Instead, the tourist guide arranges and organizes its statements according to a mode of succession—or perhaps accumulation—that is entirely characteristic. The series of statements in each section, like the division of the information itself, are not in a relation of enunciative dependency on a speaking "I"; they are listed without any thematic or narrative cohesion so that any reader can be constructed as a potential traveler by occupying the subjective position of the "I" who sees.

Recalling Walter Benjamin's discussion of information in the "Story-teller," the new representational character of the tourist guide corresponds to the shift from experience to information as the "new" mode of communication. The rise of the tourist guide occurred during an era when the dissemination of information through the media, such as newspapers, public notices, and governmental reports like the Blue Books, achieved its cultural dominance. No longer was knowledge mediated through the experience of a particular subject. The new mode of knowledge was defined by the accumulation of "informative" statements uttered in a dispersive fashion.[13]

As a body of information about the Orient, the tourist guide, like the journalistic statement, borrows its authority from a claim to verifiability, not from the experience of a speaking subject. What is at stake here is the *constructability* of the discourse. The tourist guide encourages its readers to check, to confirm or deny the validity of the information it provides, because it is precisely this acknowledgment of the possibility of error that makes the tourist believe what the guide claims, while perpetuating, of course, a circular system of exchanging information.

In such an excessively informational discourse, the statements can only be descriptive, for representation cannot claim to be mediated through a specific agent; it has to hold a mediating relation between the tourist and other sources of information. Recognizing "the absence in Eastern countries of those local records and public notices which are to be found in every town and village of the West," the handbook encourages its consumer—making the tourist feel almost morally obligated—to become an information collector and join its mechanisms for revision and reproduction.[14] The will to verify, if I may call it that, has the effect of internalizing information gathering as a touristic activity. The guide constructs its reading subject as someone who participates in a positivistic, empiricist operation of "verifying" existing information, which, needless to say, has strategic value in maintaining colonial power as well as "scientific" value in "mapping" the Orient for the West.

In such a circular system of exchange between the tourist and the guide, information becomes a valorized form of knowledge that requires no interpretation or further explanation for it to be communicated. Here it is empirical accuracy that counts—as opposed to interpretation or "making sense" in the case of the travelogue. The mere listing of statements in an accumulative fashion and their constant modification and correction through an all-inclusive process of revision by the users are the very guarantee of its communicability and truthfulness. Information, Benjamin acutely points out, is "understandable in itself."[15]

Such an informational mode of knowledge relies heavily on what Foucault calls "grids of specification" to present its statement. Whereas the travelogue as an autobiographical discourse often constructs its narrative around the general experience of its heroic traveler, expecting the reader to fill in the narrative gaps through a kind of identification with the narrator, the discourse of tourism is obsessed with ways of specifying the knowledge it provides, thus attempting to cover every possible point of information about the Orient. Each section of both Quetin's guide and Murray's handbooks begins with an introduction divided into subsections with information on modes of traveling; traveling servants; accommodations for travelers; the appropriate presents for representatives of the local government (i.e., bribes); charts of monetary exchange, and weights and measures; the "character" of the natives—their manners, customs, and religion; and a useful vocabulary. These are followed by descriptions of the cities, their specific geographical locations, tourist sights, detailed information about the roads and their conditions, the specific length of time needed to travel them, and so on.

The tourist guide is thus a "hysterical" discourse characterized by an excess of specification, almost to the point of informational "prattle"—to use Barthes's term[16]—suggesting its fear of incompleteness, or perhaps of failure to communicate. To avoid incompleteness, it packs layers of information in ways that leave no space for interpretation or possible misunderstanding. The description of Gomati, a small, perhaps even insignificant village on the road between Salonica and Mount Athos, is an excellent example of the grid of specification:

> Gomati, a village scattered among fruit trees and gardens, in the middle of a narrow steep valley with abrupt and wooded sides. As this Valley descends towards the S., it spreads into a circular basin hemmed in by low and rounded hills, beyond which appear in the distance the sea and the cone of Mount Athos. Gomati formerly consisted of 230 houses. It has now only 130, 70 of which are exempt from taxation. From Gomati, the road descends through the valley into the basin below. 2½ hours brings the traveller to the brow overlooking the Strymonic Gulf, where a new prospect opens at every step, composed of dark foregrounds, with light and airy distances varied by stupendous mountains, and picturesque rocks. At the feet lies the track of the canal, through which the fleets of Xerxes steered; the mountains of Magnesia and Pieria are to the W., while N. and E. are Pangeus and the Mountains of Macedonia. (Murray's *Hand-Book for Travellers in the Ionian Islands*, 249–50)

I have quoted this description at length to demonstrate the tourist guide's tendency to prattle. Not only are the details concerning the agricultural and geographical state of the small village described, the guide even provides such seemingly unimportant data as the number of households and taxpayers and the hypothetical piece of information about the fleets of Xerxes crossing the canal. Such specifications are not so much an acknowledgment of the tourist's need for a detailed description of what he or she may want to see—though they are perhaps helpful for a business person or a government agent—as they are the sign of an obsession with absolute completeness. The tourist guide is a discourse that has to expend itself through overproduction of detailed information to achieve a sense of totality, perhaps because it lacks the unifying role of an author-traveler. Since it cannot derive its sense of completion from the central presence of an author, the tourist guide must accumulate details to fill the empty spaces in its divided, categorized, and classified information.[17]

The most symptomatic manifestation of the tendency to specify and to classify information appears in the tourist guide's excessive use of maps, charts, and tables. Detailed maps of every geographical location, diagrams of such obscure matters as the ideal shape of the apparatus of the traveler's sleeping tent, and charts and tables of every classifiable piece of information—from steamer fares, schedules, and the distances between every two possible locations, to monetary exchange rates and even such insignificant information as the revenue of the Knights of Malta at their expulsion in 1789—are furnished. These guides sometimes even include drawings of the sights, as if tourists could not see for themselves. These hyperorganized bodies of information, useful though they may seem to the tourist, point to an empirical pseudoscientific tradition that valorizes "a corpuscular atomic theory of knowledge and information," as Johannes Fabian has said of anthropological research.[18] Like modern anthropology, the tourist guide constantly attempts to provide a "diagrammatic representation" of the experience of the tour through the Orient. The tourist is encouraged, through looking at maps, diagrams of the sights, and exact geographical descriptions, to perceive his or her position in spatial terms and to gain visual knowledge of the location. These devices encourage the tourist to visualize the Other's culture in a specific way. This method of observation, as an extension of the rationalistic and empirical bias toward "graphic-spatial conceptualization," suggests a "denial of coevalness or temporalization" between the European tourist and the native, because the former has to view the Orient outside its sociohistorical context. In other words, the discourse of tourism frames the Orient and the Oriental tour in geographical and spatial terms without any views of its sociohistorical situation. Even when the tourist guide does provide a "history" of the location, it is often an account of its *past* glory; as it brushes aside the colonial reality of the present state. By concentrating on present geographical features and past images of the Orient, the guide denies the natives any coevalness in the context of the tourist's encounter with them and discourages the tourist from trying to understand the implications of such an ideological voyage. History here is provided so as to distance the Other, not to bring him or her closer to the European tourist. The tourist guide pretends that its description is eternal by defining a historical "past" to which the Orient and its inhabitants are exiled and a geographical "present" where the tourist and his or her Oriental experience are located. Even though the guide is constantly being revised and updated, which logically makes its textuality temporary and not eternally fixed, its discourse persists in promoting the eternalization of the object. The geospatial discourse of the guide erases all the traces of how the Orient reached its current situation or became available to the European tourist. As a discourse of power, the guidebook is, in other words, on the side of amnesia. Although the guide marks a transformation of the travelogue's rules of formation, it does not generate new theoretical and ideological choices. In fact, its informational vision of the Other continues to make possible the "commodification" of the Orient for tourists belatedly searching for the disappearing exotic—that is to say, the guidebook encourages the notion that the Orient just happens to be there for the use of the tourist-consumer.

Tourism, Colonialism, and the Guide

In The Archaeology of Knowledge Michel Foucault points out that since a discourse is a practice, and not merely a group of signs or statements, its authority must depend on its function in a "field of non-discursive practices [un champ de pratiques non-discursives]" (68). For example, the discourse of general grammar had in the eighteenth century an important function in pedagogic practice, and the analysis of wealth played a significant role not only in the government's political decisions but also in the quotidian practices of capitalism. For the tourist guide, the field of non-discursive practice is the large tourist industry and the colonial administration as parts of the capitalist economy. The second set of questions I raised at the outset concerning the ideological status of the discursive formation of tourist guides and the political implications of the shift in orientalist travel literature from travelogue to tourist guide can be addressed only in connection with the newborn capitalist practice of tourism, which worked hand in hand with the colonial enterprise to absorb the exotic into European economies.

Yet, given the complexities and ambivalences of the tourist guide and its supporting industry, the discursive shifts I have studied entail the potential for positive changes in the relations of colonial power and yet changes that can be recuperated by the very same relations to exploit the Orient further. The shift from travelogue to tourist guide constitutes a moment of discursive *slippage* where one can locate both transformational possibilities in Orientalism and strategies of affirmation, which work together in a complementary fashion to make room for the desire for the Orient and the exercise of colonial power. Let me discuss these ideological splits that the guide engenders in more detail.

First, to the extent that the tourist guide transforms the orientalist savant into a sightseer by turning the (institutionalized) Oriental site of investigation into a "sight," it has a potential for discursive transformation or even oppositionality. For, if one agrees with Said, Fabian, and Clifford that the relation between the European subject of knowledge and the Other as the object of his or her study is a "relationship of power, of domination, of varying degrees of a complex hegemony," then the problematization of such a relationship is a positive development, at least for the Orientals.[19] This is not to privilege sight-seeing over orientalist observation and the practice of signification; nor is it to claim that since the rise of tourism every orientalist has become a sightseer. But orientalist tourism and its discourse can and in some cases do imply—and in fact generate—a new relation between the European traveler and the Oriental in which the former is not an egotistical subject of knowledge and the latter is not an object of institutional investigation. Unlike the orientalist traveler, the tourist is less concerned with *capturing* the exotic signified than with "sliding" over the signifiers of otherness. In other words, what brings the tourist to the Orient is not the "lordly" attempts of earlier orientalists to understand and "make sense" of the internal dynamics of Oriental culture and to gain "new" knowledge about them, but the desire to identify the already defined signs of exoticism as exotic. Although the promotion of the Oriental culture as an "exotic" commodity is intertwined with the relations of colonial power, as I will discuss shortly, the discourse of tourism suggests a passage in orientalist vision from perceiving the Orient as the object of cultural domination to seeing it as an object of desire.

In the context of this change, harsh criticism of orientalist tourism by such great travelers as Pierre Loti (in *Jérusalem* and *La Mort de Philae*), Maurice Barrès (in *Une enquête aux pays du Levant*), and others can be viewed as an indication of the way the new industry problematized the status of the orientalist and depreciated the value of his or her experience and the resultant travelogue.[20] To use Flaubert's definition in the *Dictionnaire des idées reçues*, the orientalist simply became a "man who has traveled a lot [un homme qui a beaucoup voyagé]."

No longer is the Oriental journey an exclusive enterprise for the privileged few whose egotistical will to knowledge led them to the Orient in search of new discoveries. Rather it has become an "ordinary," leisurely vacation that anyone can take to escape the daily routine of European life and to indulge in the desire for the Orient. The discourse and practice of tourism also imply the "leveling" of the differences between the Orient and the Occident. I have used the term *tourist guide* throughout this chapter without any specific qualification to suggest that much of what I have said about the discursive formation of the orientalist tourist guide can also be said of guides for European cities and countries. Indeed, in the mid-nineteenth century there were many guides for France, Italy, Switzerland, and Spain, places that were more popular as tourist resorts than the Orient by reason of their proximity and comfort. There is no place outside the domain of the tourist industry; every city, country, or region has the potential of being packaged and commodified as a site for tourism. In such a hegemonic enterprise, there is little difference between, say, Cairo and London, or Constantinople and Paris. As far as the discourse that represents these cities and the tourist who visits them are concerned, they are all different from home, even though a European in a city such as Paris can be simultaneously "inside" and "outside" it, which is not true for Cairo.

And yet, to the extent that the tourist guide and the desire for the Orient that it produces are mediated by colonial power relations, the transformational possibilities also mark a strategic reconfiguration of Europe's domination of its Other. The leveling of differences between Oriental and Occidental resorts by the tourist industry and its discourse, one may go on to argue, attests less to a balancing of power between Europe and its Other than to a hegemonic dissolution of the Orient in the complex power network of European capitalism and colonialism. On the one hand, the Orient as a commodity in the tourist industry has dissolved into Europe since it is no longer "outside" Europe's economic and power relations. On the other hand, the Orient has been invaded by colonialist and capitalist enterprises, and so has become a site for European military and commercial operations. As a phenomenon of the most advanced stage of European colonialism, the tourist industry can thus be considered a kind of militarism that violates the Orient culturally and economically by extending Europe's domination. As the category of "colon" in the subtitle of Quetin's guide for Algeria suggests, colonialist interests are inseparable from those of the tourist industry. Reflecting on his departure from Cairo, Nerval makes the following insightful remarks: "That old Cairo lived under ash and dust; modern spirit and progress have triumphed over it like death [l'esprit et les progrès modernes en ont triomphé comme la mort]. Only a few more months and the European-styled streets would cut in right angles the old dusty and mute city, peacefully crumbling on to the poor Fellahs. What shines, what glitters, what grows is the French quarter, the Italian, Provençal, and Maltese districts, the future warehouse of British India" (1:296). Although Nerval's mourning can be interpreted as an orientalist's nostalgia for a "pure" Orient, it does point nonetheless to the cultural and economic invasion of the Orient by European colonizers. Nerval's prophecy had come true by the time Loti wrote his *La Mort de Philae* (1908), in which he describes how the "offensive intrusion" of the tourist industry brought about "the death of Cairo."[21] Loti describes how the "new invaders [nouveaux envahisseurs]" (the "Cooks and Cookesses," as he calls them elsewhere) violate Egyptian culture by their disrespectful behavior in the mosques, temples, and classical monuments. Loti, of course, does not point out the more prominent aspects of such an intrusion, but there is abundant evidence of the economic invasion; for example, in Joanne's guides for the Oriental cities, all of which begin with a series of advertisements for tourist hotels owned by European colonizers (figure 3). This is not to say that tourism is solely responsible for the invasion. But as a capitalist phenomenon, the tourist industry creates a new market and generates new businesses that are monopolized by European colonizers at the cost of the native culture and economy. As Susan Buck-Morss has pointed out, "tourism prostitutes a culture, in the very bourgeois sense of money exchange."[22] Thus, what glitters in Cairo, what grows in Algiers, what shines in Tunis are the European quarters, whose development implies the quiet crumbling of the old cities and their cultures on top of the impoverished natives.

Furthermore, as a product of the most advanced stage of Orientalism, the tourist guide itself has an important ideological function in relation to the practices and strategies of power involved in European colonialism. Above all, the tourist guide can be viewed as an ultimate instrument of knowledge (and therefore power) that mediates the relation of the traveler to the sight. As the word *handbook* suggests, the large body of orientalist knowledge, once a heavy burden on the traveler's shoulders, now presents itself as a *vade-mecum*, a helping hand, to be held in the hand and

Figure 3. Hotel advertisement. Reproduced by permission of Editions Robert Laffont.

to be carried by every traveler as an ordinary travel accessory. A discursive formation such as the tourist guide attests to the inception of a *systematic* stage of orientalist knowledge in which methods of encountering and observing the Other are now systematically packaged as the book to be used uniformly in the field by every traveler, from the *savant* to the worldly man, from the artist to the colonizer. This eliminates the possibility of deviation from the orientalist point of view while simultaneously positing various subject positions for the traveling reader.

In this sense, the tourist guide marks a new and more dominant stage in the evolution of Orientalism. As a guiding manual, the tourist guide offers the tourist a fully programmed approach to the Orient, mapping a suitable itinerary, designating the appropriate sights, determining the proper activities, and, indeed, defining the desire for the Orient. In short, the tourist guide as a *practice* that allows the interplay of relations among orientalist institutions, the economic interests involved in the tourist industry, and the sociocultural processes that determine a desire for Oriental exoticism perpetuates and strengthens the dominant ideology of orientalist knowledge through the implantation and dissemination of its informational apparatus.

3. Notes on Notes, or with *Flaubert* in Paris, Egypt

✸

Writing on Flaubert's travel notes is ineluctably a practice of note taking: his disparate text demands a kind of aphoristic response that does not close on the signified but allows a movement of disconnection and variation. This dispersed chapter thus does not pretend to be anything other than a series of notes initially jotted down in Paris, where I read the original notes of Flaubert's journey to Egypt (1849–50)—*carnets* 4 and 5—and then rewritten in the United States a few months later. This *double*, or revisionary, writing involves displacement both in time and place: writing in two different times and places and writing as the reinscription of an earlier writing.

My double writing parallels Flaubert's own *double écriture*, and it is therefore conscious of its own duplicity: this writing is not only reflective but complicitous. On the one hand, my notes read as a kind of rewriting of the orientalist notes of Flaubert and so engage in an orientalist practice. When I was studying Flaubert's original notes in the Bibliothèque Historique in Paris, trying to decipher his faded handwriting, I could not stop thinking how much my scholarly activity paralleled Flaubert's orientalist act of note taking in and on Egypt; or perhaps, even more disturbing, it resembled the garrulous Orientalism of Maxime Du Camp!

And yet, reading Flaubert's orientalist notes as an "Oriental" did not leave me indifferent to its politics of representation—for a moment, the text raised the possibility that I could have been the object of Flaubert's gaze and representation. Conscious of my own displacement—writing always away from the Orient, away from home—and of the duplicitous nature of my note taking, I rewrote my earlier "rewriting" so that it became a critique of Flaubert: a perverse turning *against* the text in this instance—I say "perverse" because this move splits my writing on Flaubert between a kind of duplicitous identification with and a critical differentiation from his discursive practice.

My notes do not always succeed in engaging in such a critical, self-conscious practice. They testify not only to my complicitous position but also to the impossibility for me of an "outside" view of Orientalism from which I could criticize its political economy. Does not the act of writing about the European discourse on the Orient unwittingly imply and involve itself in an orientalist practice? My notes thus take the form of a critical drift that allows the writing to speak its double discourse, its duplicitous relation with the "original" notes: I rewrote critically my own writing of Flaubert's notes and his rewriting of the Oriental experience in a place and for an audience away from the Orient.

Fragments of a Belated Orientalist's Discourse

Flaubert's Notes de voyages provided me with the fragments of a belated orientalist's discourse.[1] Whereas Nerval in his Voyage en Orient announces nostalgically the disappearance of the orientalist savant, Flaubert declares in melancholia the emergence of the belated orientalist whose split identity imposes a diffracted discourse.[2] His telegraphic notes written down during his journey to Egypt and then rewritten in France—clearly for his own pleasure, for he never intended to publish them—constitute the threshold of a dispersed, heterogeneous Orientalism that can be articulated only as a self-conscious, utterly perverse discourse of discontent(ment).[3] Soon after his arrival in Egypt, Flaubert abandoned the idea of writing an organized travelogue like those of his orientalist precursors: "I had the intention of writing in this way about my journey, in paragraphs, in the form of little chapters, as soon as I had the time. This was not feasible; I had to give it up as soon as the Khamsin [the Egyptian sandstorm] had arrived and we could stick our nose out" (Notes, 437). For the belated traveler, Oriental reality is a simoom, a violently hot, dry dust storm that blurs his vision and disorients his sense of order. The dust storm flusters his will to represent, making him renounce his desire for a systematic account of his journey.

The belated orientalist's discourse is thus an antinarrative, a discursive constellation without a shape, an ideological practice without a doctrine. Such a discourse refuses to be integrated into a whole and can be traced only in the fragmentary reflections of an ambivalent traveler who finds the place of his or her displacement and the locus of his or her discontent in the Orient. The belated orientalist journey is always a dis-Orient-ation,[4] for the search for a "counterexperience" in the Other turns out to be a discovery of its loss and the absence of an alternative.

Yet, it is precisely this articulation of the loss as a discourse of discontentment that differentiates the belated orientalist's discourse from the official (dominant) modes of orientalist representation that can never be obliterated. Flaubert's text does not and cannot attempt to subvert the dominant discourse, but it *disfigures* it by taking it to the limit of its representational power and exposing its contradictions. The belated traveler is a duplicitous figure who appropriates the dominant discourse but exceeds its ideological assumptions by his or her perversion, unsettles its order by producing noise in its system, and disturbs its consciousness by giving voice to its unconscious.

As a plural text, Flaubert's *Notes de voyages* refuses to be constrained by a structured form of criticism that could decipher its meaning—for one thing, there is no semantic unity here—but demands instead a kind of interpretive drift that would allow the text's plurality to be constituted: the text says, "Don't comment on me, but write with me in my perverse fashion."[5] My reading therefore does not attempt to explain the meaning of Flaubert's journey to Egypt; nor does it try to expound his "brand" of Orientalism. Rather, my interpretation will involve a dissipation that "explodes" the text without exhausting it. The operating principle here is not semantic finality or discursive totality but a mode of interpretation that recognizes and accepts the disturbing orderlessness and fracturedness of the modern text.

To read as such is not to ignore the political implications of Flaubert's ideological journey. Like every text, his *Notes* comes with its "sociolect" and "ideolect,"[6] which like a shadow follow the text everywhere. The aim of my interpretive drift is precisely to reflect on the text's complicated relation with its shadow by exposing the seam that simultaneously splits and joins the opposing ideological forces which are in a state of becoming in the discourse of the belated orientalist. The interpretive drift is a way of cutting the text without rendering it abstract; it consists of perforating the text's surface in order to grasp its complexity.[7]

Silence

In Egypt, Flaubert discovered the aesthetics of silence, the practice of nonrepresentation. Initially, he undertook the journey to fill the "blank notebooks" that he had kept under "quadruple cachet" after his first trip to Corsica (*Notes*, 438). The blank sheets later came to signify the vacuity, the absence of the exotic referent that could only be found elsewhere, in an *Other* journey. The Oriental trip was therefore taken in the spirit of an escapist search for a mode of representation devoid of the sterility and banality characteristic of the dominant discourses of mid-nineteenth-century France. The journey was meant to act as an antidote to his intellectual ennui, just as the warm climate was to treat his nervous disorder.

And yet, ironically, Flaubert abandoned writing on his arrival in Egypt. In a letter to Louis Bouilhet, he says, "The first few days, I started to write a bit, but thank God, I quickly recognized the ineptitude—it's better to be quite simply an eye" (*Lettres*, 237). Representational ineptitude imposes itself immediately on the belated traveler to the Orient, rendering him incapable of recording the differences he can only observe—*being* (sight) instead of *doing* (discourse). The encounter with the Other made Flaubert realize that in a time when everyone spoke garrulously, in a world where every discourse was a form of infinite prattle, to be quiet was a form of oppositional art. His cotraveler, Maxime Du Camp, provided him with a living example of a garrulous orientalist who never refrained from representing the Orient through his daguerreotypes and published accounts of his journey. Flaubert reacted against his type by practicing nonrepresentation, for he understood unwittingly, but correctly, that silence could be a subversive gesture in a noisy system. He defied through his *active* withholding of discourse the cultural expectation that a writer of his status should necessarily write about his "experience" in the Orient. Flaubert's silence was not a mere failure to speak; he retained his words intentionally.

For him, silence was not the negation of writing but the effect of its excess. The orientalist prattle manifested in the texts he took with him, or read before his journey—Edward W. Lane's *Modern Egyptians*, Lamartine's *Voyage en Orient*, Volney's *Voyage en Syrie et en Egypte*, for example—imposed a state of verbosity that discomfited him to the point of oppositional inarticulateness. Why speak when there is already a plethora of orientalist utterances? Why write when writing can only reproduce that *already*?

And yet, Flaubert *did* write, but "aphonically": he whispered his memories of the Orient to himself in a diary, the most private form of representation. He rewrote his notes but refused to publish them, so allowing his desire for orientalist representation to be muffled in an empty space—talking to/for himself in privacy.

His discursive diffidence made him appreciate the silence of the desert more than any other traveler did, for it offered him the experience of the void, the presence of the absence, a space where solitude and silence made the production of meaning impossible. He wandered alone for hours in the Abou-Solôme Desert, contemplating its "silent immobility, the grandeur without movement" (*carnet* 4, 5 1v).

The desert is the evasive listener that provokes a crisis in the orientalist's relation to representation: Flaubert could only repeat the word *silence* in the desert.[8] The desert is the brink of the Oriental reality; once reached, it throws the orientalist into a discursive void, into dead silence.

Flânerie

In the Orient, the modern traveler maintains his European habit of strolling. Whether in the barren desert, where he can contemplate emptiness, or in the city, where he is able to witness the "Oriental" phantasmagoria, the belated orientalist is a *flâneur*, an idler who tries to see more of the Orient through his erratic sauntering and by remaining dependent on chance. Always guided by a dragoman and feeling restrained by his ushering, Flaubert craved disorientation. Drifting alone haphazardly provided him with such an occasion: "I walk all alone in Cairo, under the beautiful sunshine, . . . I get lost in alleyways and reach dead ends. From time to time, I find a square made from the debris of homes, or rather houses which are missing; hens peck about, cats are on the walls—tranquil life, warm and secluded" (*Notes*, 475). Even though he enjoyed the security of an organized trip, Flaubert was bored by its regimented structure. Strolling without a guide in the labyrinthine city allowed him to experience, for a moment, the lost pleasures of loss and "discovery," pleasures denied to him as a belated traveler. Like Nerval, Flaubert expected the Orient to be the scene of the otherness he had dreamed of in his childhood; he wanted to find himself in an unknown neighborhood, a place where he could get lost, come to dead ends, and feel displaced. Flaubert did not look for orientalist *connaissance*, he went after Oriental *méconnaissance*.

Flânerie suits the amateur traveler because it also caters to his desire to be "all eye," to have a penetrating gaze without socializing. The joy of watching exceeded any other pleasure for Flaubert: "Bazars.—Café where I spend almost all afternoon, looking at people, a burial takes place in the square" (*Notes*, 520). The modern orientalist is not in a hurry to accomplish anything; he is a leisurely traveler satisfied with his indolence and inertia; he lets the scene of otherness act on him to the point of intoxication, which makes him finally move. Flaubert wanted to absorb the Orient in himself by looking: "I was gorging myself with colors like a donkey filling itself with oats [je me foutais une ventrée de couleurs, comme un âne s'emplit d'avoine]" (*Lettres*, 118). The belated orientalist is a *voracious* observer.

Without a knowledge of Arabic, Flaubert was excluded from the symbolic domain, which made him obsessively attached to the Other's imaginary, the visual realm of image repertoire: "We walk in the desert, we sleep on the ground, without any idea, almost speechless; a good day of idleness and air. On the high ground, in view of the Citadel, an old mosque. We climb the ruined steps of the old minaret from where one can almost see Cairo, the old Cairo almost on the first level, the two tall white minarets of Mohammed Ali's mosque, the pyramids, Sakkarah, the valley of the Nile, the desert beyond, Choubra below to the right" (*Notes*, 469). The orientalist flâneur strives for the unobstructed panoramic view—to see more space in less time. Such a view indulged Flaubert, the belated traveler, in his imperialist fantasy of all-seeing as a way of embracing the Other in its totality—in a time of fragmentation and incoherence. What matters here is not the details of the scene but its wide perspective, which helped Flaubert "capture" the whole of Egypt in a flash.

The tendency to have a wide angle of vision is symptomatic of the modern orientalist's fragmentation. Since he can no longer achieve a sense of epistemological totality, he indulges in a scopophilic desire that situates him in a panoptic position from which he can have a panoramic view. The more Flaubert became conscious that he was a tourist passing by, the more he desired an overview of the itinerant space that he never achieved. The belated orientalist is a "mounted" flâneur who sees a tourist panorama without the overview of the geographer.

As a result, the modern orientalist's discourse is caught between (cut by?) a desire to depict the local color as *sketches* and the tendency to capture the *whole* experience in a diary. Read individually, each entry is a sketch that the orientalist flâneur jotted down in flight. Viewed in their totality, the notes are a synoptic account of a modern journey. On the one hand, the pleasure of a discursive drift, the recognition of discontinuity, the repudiation of the whole, the scene of the intractable; on the other hand, the power of totality, the triumph of completeness, the mastery of full representation.

Transvestism

The belated orientalist is a cultural transvestite. Bored with the European redingote, the gloomy black frock coat that felt like an urban uniform, Flaubert adopted the Egyptian costume as soon as he arrived in Cairo (figure 4). "Following the unanimous advice of sensible people," he wrote proudly to his mother, "I am dressed in flannel waistband, flannel shirt, flannel underpants, cloth trousers, a large vest, a fat tie, and cardigan on the top of my vest at night and in the morning—I am shaved and wear a red tarboosh with two white little bonnets underneath" (*Lettres*, 140). Like most orientalists, Flaubert wore Oriental clothes for strategic reasons, to facilitate his journey. Attentive to the "sensible" advice of other experienced travelers, he wanted to be taken as an Oriental so that he could visit holy shrines and obscure places from which Europeans were excluded. In this sense, the Oriental costume was a disguise, a kind of orientalist masquerade that hid the truth of Flaubert's Europeanness so that he could see more of the Orient.

Yet, Flaubert's description of his costume conveys a sense of excess manifested most clearly in his vestimentary hypertrophy—or fanatic transvestism—which expresses also his desire to *be* the Other. Everything from his underwear to the red tarbooch with two little white bonnets had to be Egyptian. For the belated traveler, the Other's costume offers a visible locus of transformation through which he can practice self-exoticism: Flaubert wanted to reconstruct his self as an (Oriental) Other through his transvestism.

Costume poses the problem of identity: to wear Oriental clothes is both a way of renouncing one's identity and a form of conversion to the Other's imaginary. Orientalist transvestism suggests the suspension of reality, the desire to liberate oneself from the European sameness symptomatically manifested in the gloomy redingote. Flaubert viewed his orientalist transvestism as a form of cultural resistance to his Europeanness, a mode of self-fashioning through which he constituted his desired image: the Other absorbed in himself. Flaubert did not want simply to *be* in Egypt, he wished to *live* it through his transvestism: "Here we are in Egypt. . . . We are here and we live here, with a head more shaved than a knee, smoking long pipes and drinking coffee on divans" (*Notes*, 171). The traveler's emphasis on *living* in Egypt, as opposed to simply being there, underlines his mimetic desire for identification. But there is a clear sense of naiveté in

Figure 4. Flaubert the cultural transvestite. Photo by Maxime Du Camp.

Flaubert's desire to live like an Oriental as he equates here the Other's culture with his shaved head and long pipes. And yet, was not Flaubert's cultural naiveté what liberated him from the orientalist savant, the subject of power and knowledge in him?

The Other's imaginary absorbed Flaubert's attention to the point of making him identify with the Other in his image repertoire. His Orient was a world of visual inscriptions: people, gestures, signs, drawings. Unlike the orientalist savant, he did not seek essences; nor did he question the truth of appearances: a love of signs without essential content. Instead of keeping his ideological distance from the Other, the belated orientalist dissolves himself in images, figures, and signs of otherness, allowing the abolition of observer and observed, subject and object, self and Other.

Souvenir

Flaubert often recorded the purchase of his souvenirs, the Oriental objects he bought and collected while traveling—notes such as "bought some belts and amulets" (Notes, 500); "leaving the temple, bought two spears" (*Notes*, 507); "Promenade in Assouan, purchasing of a silver ring from a bread merchant" (*Notes*, 515). The belated orientalist is a souvenir collector; he purchases many objects during his journey to remind himself later of his *past* experience of the Orient. The souvenir is therefore a nostalgic object,[9] something whose presence can only testify to the loss of something experienced in an irretrievable past: the presence of what is absent. The souvenir, as the etymology of the word suggests, constitutes a trace—a memory or a reminder (*mémoire*)—of an authentic experience that must be left behind.

The souvenir is also a metonymic object in that it substitutes a part for the whole. The fragmentary objects the orientalist traveler buys take the place of the whole of his or her Oriental experience, and therefore they must always remain partial to his or her journey. The metonymic structure of the souvenir makes it a kind of fetish, for the substituted object is overvalued to the point of replacing the whole (figure 5). Unable to possess the whole of the Other, the fetishistic traveler derives pleasure from appropriating a part of it: "I buy two locks of women's hair with their ornaments" (*Notes*, 510); "we bought not women, but their underpants [nous . . . avons acheté pas des femmes mais des pagnes (= leur caleçons)]" (*Lettres*, 252–53). To buy the Oriental woman's lock of hair, to own her underwear, is to feel in possession of her body. Yet this kind of appropriation implies dispossession, for the fetishist clearly knows that what he possesses is a mere substitute for what he cannot have—note the ironic acknowledgment of "nous avons acheté *pas* des femmes." The fetishistic souvenir is thus the material sign of the lack, the metonymic symbol of dispossession.

But the desire to accumulate Oriental objects also makes the belated traveler a kind of orientalist antiquarian who attempts to reconstruct an "imaginary" past through the materiality of the objects collected. Distressed and nostalgic about the disappearance of the indigenous Oriental culture under the web of Western colonial power, Flaubert tried to preserve it for himself by appropriating its surviving metonymic objects. He concretized the historical reality of the Oriental experience by collecting its artifacts, the remnants of its decaying culture.

Flaubert was determined and tenacious in finding these "authentic" objects: "We go all the way to the end of the village to purchase a Nubian lyre" (*Notes*, 505). The search for authenticity, for a signifier of the "true" Orient, is a critical part of the belated orientalist's practice of collecting, for he recognizes the increasingly mediated and abstracted nature of his

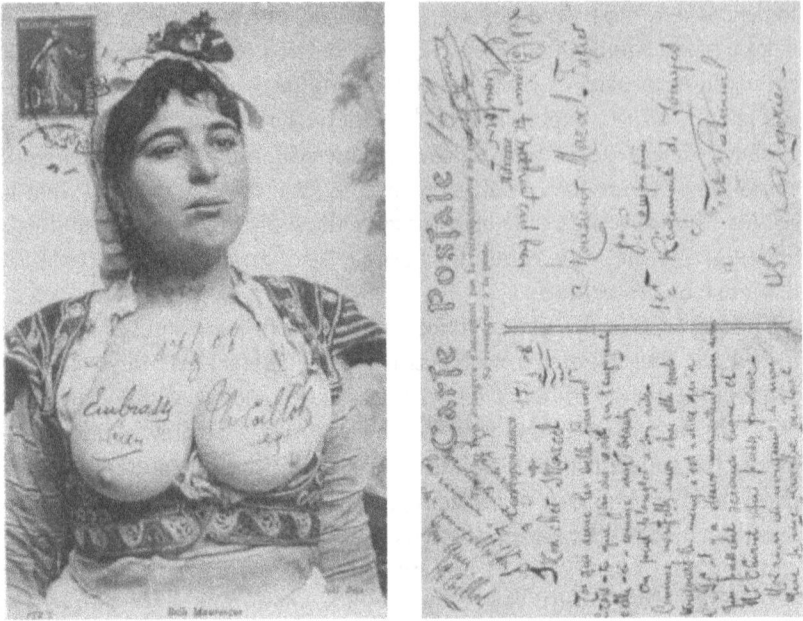

Figure 5. Souvenir du voyage!?

modern journey and the unoriginality of his Oriental experience. He tries to remedy this lack by searching for the authentic object. The souvenir provides a context of origin which authenticates the traveler's relation to the exotic Other and its experience, and to a personal past that signifies the Orient's elapsed existence.

While the material presence of the souvenir authenticates the experience of the journey, its dislocation renders it meaningless, for the souvenir is a displacement of the event, and it implies a movement from the real to the imaginary. The orientalist traveler takes the Oriental objects away from their original setting to the private space of his or her European home, transforming them into ornamental objects of exoticism.[10] Such an exotic object is an abstraction of its value and context, the estrangement of a piece from the totality of its lived relations. Flaubert decorated his rooms with such decontextualized objects: "His office . . . was very large, decorated only with books, a few portraits of friends and some souvenirs of trips; the dried corpses of young caimans, a mummy's foot . . . , amber-colored Oriental beads, a gilded Buddha, . . . on the floor, on one side, an immense Turkish divan covered with cushions, on the other side, a magnificent hide of a white bear."[11] The orientalist's room is a model of the

Orient. Through his collection of souvenirs, Flaubert interiorized both the exteriority of the Orient and his own Oriental experience. Such a transformation implies the death of the "original" object and the disappearance of its historical context—the dried bodies of the caimans and the mummified foot symbolize here the stasis of Oriental history for the belated traveler. Although the souvenir's referent is authenticity, in the private space of the orientalist's office there is no historical continuity between the object and its referent. Here the souvenir marks the erasure of history—both the Orient's historical reality and the traveler's own temporal experience—and the creation of a new history: the modern traveler's nostalgic narrative of an imaginary Orient.

Only in a room full of Oriental souvenirs could Flaubert remember his journey and rewrite his *Notes de voyages*. For Flaubert, rewriting his notes was also a souvenir, a material way of remembering his Oriental journey.

Ethnography/Tourism

Flaubert was split between being a tourist and acting as an amateur ethnographer. His discourse is divided between the leisurely notes of an ordinary traveler and an exhaustive description of Egyptian culture. On a conscious level, while completely ignoring his official mission of collecting information for the Ministère de l'Agriculture et du Commerce,[12] he viewed his journey as a leisurely stepping outside the familiar reality of home, a pleasurable liberation from the boredom of his daily European life. The emphasis on leisure is a common theme in his letters from Egypt: "We are leading a good life, poor dear old woman.— . . . if you only knew the calmness around us and in what peaceful profundity one feels the spirit roaming—we laze around, we saunter, we daydream. . . . I am getting fat in a revolting fashion" (*Lettres*, 215–16); "we travel slowly for the rest of our journey, not tiring ourselves and spending a long time watching [regardant avec de longues contemplations] everything that passes us on the Nile, sleeping a lot, fattening up like pigs, and having a charmingly ruddy tan" (*Lettres*, 230). The belated traveler is neither a heroic adventurer like his romantic precursors nor a serious explorer of cultural differences and empirical knowledge like the orientalist savant. Rather he is a pleasure seeker who takes the time to enjoy his vacation, allowing things to happen to and for himself. Even Flaubert's *longues contemplations* could not undermine his corporal relation to the Orient; he always privileged the body over the mind, letting it pursue the pleasure principle.

As a hedonistic traveler, the tourist is a consumer of sights and a passive observer of the already seen: "Clump of palm trees surrounded by small circular walls, at the foot of which two Turks were smoking; it was like an engraving, an image of the Orient in a book" (495); "Bet-Quali: (see the description of the young Champollion in his *Lettres sur la Nubie*)" (*Notes*, 512). The touristic vision is an "inauthentic" experience of déjà vu mediated through the orientalist intertext that has already identified and coded the signs of exoticism for the viewer. The belated orientalist thus cannot avoid surrendering his or her "immediate" encounter with the Other to the impression of an earlier visit. "Anyone who is a little attentive *re-discovers* much more than he/she *discovers* [Pour qui voit les choses avec quelqu'attention on *retrouve* encore bien plus qu'on ne *trouve*]" confesses Flaubert in a letter to Doctor Cloquet (*Lettres*, 173). There is no escape from the inauthenticity of the modern journey; for the belated orientalist knowledge is always already a *re-connaissance*. The more Flaubert pursued his quest for an "original" view of the Orient, the more he recognized his vicarious, contrived experience of the symbolic incrustation of the exotic referent.

But in such a politically charged field as Orientalism, even the unoriginal vision of the tourist can lend itself to the production of knowledge and thus be implicated in the relations of power. The leisurely quality of the tourist's gaze provides him with the best prospect for becoming an amateur ethnographer collecting empirical data about the natives and their culture. Although the Orient had been thoroughly studied by the time of Flaubert's visit, the epistemological apparatus of Orientalism always needed information collectors to supply its mechanism of revision and renewal. Of course, to a sophisticated tourist such as Flaubert, the ethnographic contemplation promised a possibility of transcending the "unoriginality" of belated orientalist experience and a way of authenticating the banality of his relation to the Other.

In the context of their discursive affiliation, Flaubert's notes thus constitute a network of ethnographic documentation. His observational acuity allowed him to take comprehensive notes on Oriental customs, ceremonies, attitudes, and habits and to meticulously record architectural and archaeological details. Flaubert's characterization of Sennaarian men is one example among many of his mastery of the ethnographic description: "The men of Sennaar are fat, but without bulging muscle structure, with a developed chest and pointed breasts like a woman. They are extremely black, with Caucasian features: small, long, delicate noses, thin lips. Their look is neither Semitic nor Negro; it is soft and malicious. The eye is entirely black except that the white of the eyes is coffee color, like the Nubians. One of them has an exostosis in the forehead and an other has one on the wrist" (*Notes*, 502). Flaubert's power of observation and his detailed cultural contextualization of this "Oriental" scene leave little to be imagined about the Sennaarian men. His description not only provides the reader with a precise portrait of the exotic Other, it also produces a physiognomic interpretation of the native's temperament that gives the characterization a sense of immediacy.

Thus, however involuntarily, as a purveyor of ethnographic knowledge Flaubert reproduced the kind of relation to the Other that he avoided as a hedonistic traveler: the orientalist as the egotistical subject of knowledge encountering the Oriental as the object of institutional investigation. While as a tourist he eluded the lordly approach of the orientalist savant "making sense" of Oriental culture, his ethnographic aspiration brought him back to the domain of the colonialist signified. Flaubert's discourse is thus the site of an ideological split: on the one hand, a transgressive desire to transcend the power relations of Orientalism through nonparticipation; and, on the other hand, the textual realization of its impossibility.

Defecation/Desecration

Throughout his journey Flaubert took a keen interest in registering the contamination of the Orient both by bird droppings and by Europeans' inscriptions. Wherever he went he vexedly encountered the marks of earlier visitors: "On the paving stones crowning the walls (roof of the temple) [of Esneh], the names of French troopers" (*Notes*, 491); "the head of Abousir [statue], in the back . . . is covered with the names of travelers" (*Notes*, 501); "a heap of hyenas' turds; every night, they come to shit there [on a temple in Maharrakah]" (*Notes*, 508); "bird shit on the ground and on the stones [in Athor temple]" (*Notes*, 519); "a white dropping of bird falls from above and spreads out [in Pylones]" (*Notes*, 523); "an inscription in pencil states that Belzoni, Stralton Beechy and Bennett were present at the opening of [the Menephta] on October 11, 1817" (*Notes*, 533), and so on. To the eyes of the belated traveler, the Orient is written on, marked by both nature (as defecation) and culture (as desecration).

At every monument Flaubert visited he found himself surrounded by the marks of European presence: "L'Europe dans l'Asie!" As a conscientious traveler, he was critical of the inscriptive waste left on the monuments by earlier European travelers. He viewed these inscriptions as cultural "disjecta," as bêtise, and compared them with bird droppings to expose their stupidity. "The inscriptions of travelers and the droppings of birds of prey are the only two ornaments of the ruin," he wrote sarcastically to Louis Bouilhet (Lettres, 287).

But beyond its manifest opposition to the European penetration, Flaubert's fascination (or frustration) with these persistent traces of the unclean and inappropriate points to the predicament of the belated orientalist's anality: his expressed preoccupation with the excretory function here represents a sublimated desire to conserve the disappearing object. The belated orientalist does not know how to lose the object he has come to find, or, more accurately, how to come to terms with the loss of the object of his desires—the disappearance of the Orient, its dissolution by European colonialism. Although Flaubert went to the Orient for self-dispossession, in search of a discontinuity with his European selfhood, once there he became retentive about the Oriental referent as he witnessed its slow disappearance under the weight of European colonialism. Arriving too late in the Orient, in a time when the Other was on the verge of being fully consumed by European hegemony, Flaubert wanted to preserve its last traces of existence; he tried to usurp what remained of the Other for himself—consider again his excessive desire to collect Oriental artifacts. He even fantasized about a trip to efface all the European inscriptions on Egyptian monuments, as if by erasing the signifiers of European penetration he could expurgate the Orient of devouring colonialism.

If Flaubert refused to write on the monuments like his precursors, it was not because he considered these travelers "thin and quite vain," as he consciously thought, but because the inscriptive disjecta meant the destruction of the Other he wanted to keep for himself. For Flaubert, writing on monuments was a material way of separating himself from the object, a way of imposing a mode of division between self and other, Occident and Orient. And yet, does not the very ironic reinscription of the European marks on the Orient in Flaubert's notes attest to the textual realization of the impossibility of such dreams of restoration and renewal?

Eventually, Flaubert realized in melancholia that the inscriptions were a waste with which, finally, he had to merge.

Abjection

Flaubert went to the Orient to find the object of his desire, the Other outside, but instead he encountered the abject in himself, inside. Filth, waste, decaying carcasses, rotten food, plague-stricken people, foul-smelling objects, stinking chancres, opened corpses: these are the images that clung to him in Egypt. Perverse as he was, Flaubert was not satisfied with the "ordinary" signs of exoticism. He passionately sought the forbidden, the intolerable, by straying into the abominable domain of abjection, the excluded locus of defilement. Abjection for him marked the crossroads of desire and disgust: "On the mat: firm flesh, bronze ass, shaved cunt, dry but fat; the whole thing gave an effect of plague and of leprosy [Sur la natte: chairs dures, cul de bronze, con rasé, sec quoique gras; l'ensemble était un effet de pestiféré et de léproserie]" (*Notes*, 458). Erotic abjection: cheap sex in a dark room on a hard floor with a plague-stricken crazy woman.[13] For Flaubert, orientalist *jouissance* demanded an abjection that simultaneously fascinated him by its otherness and wounded his identity in that the abject has recourse to castration. The sense of leprosy and plague he often experienced during sex emanated from his exposure to the domain of prohibition that forced him outside the path of his desire. Here the "con rasé" is the disturbing signifier of the absence, castration, that pulverizes his subjectivity. Abjection is a border, a kind of ambiguity that subjects the stray orientalist to his ambivalent feeling toward the Other.[14] In abjection, Flaubert was on the side of both law and prohibition, desire and repression, rejection and yearning. Caught between these opposing forces, he had no choice but to pursue the unnamable phobic object in a search that took him to the frontier of the intolerable. His peculiar visit to the Caserlaïneh hospital is a case in point: "Lovely cases of pox; in Mameluke Abbas's ward, several people had it in their asses. At a gesture of the doctor, all . . . opened their anus with their fingers to show their chancres. Enormous infundibula; one [patient] had a tuft of hair in his ass; the penis of an old man completely deprived of skin. I stepped back from the odor that emanated from it" (*Notes*, 468). Leprosy, especially on the corporeal orifices, marks the nonseparatedness, the nondistinctiveness, of the inside and the outside, which terrorizes the viewer. Flaubert recoiled in disgust, but the abject left its marks on and in him—it sickened his desire and polluted his identity. It is only through abjection that the "Oriental" can leave his marks of loathing on the orientalist consciousness. Turning his back on the colonizer and showing his stinking chancres, he says sarcastically, "Look carefully at what you came to see in the Orient!"

The exposure to the abject pulverizes the traveler's search for the object (of desire and/or knowledge) and perverts his discourse. The representations of the abject in Flaubert are the exorbitant limit of orientalist representation: a discomfiting deviation from its discursive norms, a disturbing excess of its representational power—the power of horror. Even though the images of abjection are congruous with the logic of orientalist discourse—the Orient as the unclean, the impure, the repugnant—they unsettle its order, elude its defenses, and disturb its consciousness by imposing a sense of horror that cannot be assimilated into its symbolic domain of representation.[15] The belated orientalist's encounter with the impossible realm of abjection takes him to the limit of his representation, where meaning fails him and his symbolic power collapses.

Flaubert's writing of the abject is a strange rite of defilement in a discourse of prohibition.

Sex

Unlike Nerval, Flaubert did not go to the Orient to find the "true" Oriental woman; having read Lane's *Modern Egyptians*, he knew too well that she was inaccessible. And yet, such a recognition did not stop him from pursuing the feminine object of desire in Egyptian brothels. The phantasm of Oriental sexuality, with its lure of boundless pleasure and perennial lasciviousness represented so abundantly in Western literature, made him the victim of a pathological search for the lost object. Flaubert's sexual encounters were at once affirmative and transgressive, conventional and perverse. On the one hand, like his precursors, he associated the Orient with sex and followed their exploitative habit of searching for the exotic referents of Oriental eroticism, and indulged as much as he could in their endless pleasures. His celebrated encounter with Kuchiouk-Hanem, the famous Egyptian courtesan, provides a good example of such orientalist stereotypes. The long, detailed description of his sexual exploit re-creates the imaginary scene of the harem where heavily bejeweled female bodies become the objects of male voyeurism and sexual pleasure. Kuchiouk-Hanem herself, having emerged from a refreshing bath that gave a pleasant scent of terebenthin to her "hard" bosom, is represented as the unapproachable Oriental queen wrapped in a light violet gauze that highlights the curving of her voluptuous body. As a narrative of erotic clichés, this scene does not represent so much the sexual act itself as the expectation of and the preparation for it. Flaubert's painstaking description of her exotic appearance, her opulent jewelry, is followed by a detailed account of her and the almés' "danse brutale," which eventually leads to a long evening of "the most violent fucking [baisade des plus violentes]" (*Notes*,

490). In short, the scene reaffirms the features of orientalist eroticism: the stylization of the harem, the scopic pleasure, the overabundance of jouissance, the desire for domination, the objectification of the women, their lascivious sexuality.

And yet, this and other descriptions of sexual encounters convey an ironic sense of self-consciousness that problematizes the ideological underpinnings of their thematic indulgence. For example, when he has described the final episode of his sexual encounter with Kuchiouk-Hanem, Flaubert makes two confessions: first, that sleeping with the Egyptian courtesan made him dream of "Judith and . . . Holophern sleeping together" (Notes, 490); and, second, that the whole experience reminded him of his "brothel nights in Paris" (Lettres, 245). The first comment makes apparent Flaubert's perception of his role as the oppressor who deserves to be punished by the Other. Kuchiouk-Hanem is here not only the figuration of the threat of the Other's violence but an Oriental heroine, Judith, who took her revenge on the colonizer by decapitating him. As in his cheap sex with the plague-stricken prostitute, Flaubert is once again subjected to his fear of castration in his self-identification with Holophern.

The second comment points to Flaubert's recognition of the unoriginality of his orientalist encounter, the absence of the Other erotic object, and his situation as a bourgeois consumer of (Oriental) sexuality. Here, the unapproachable, exotic Oriental queen turns out to be the familiar, accessible Parisian whore, and his experience as the omnipotent master of the harem, that of a john. Flaubert recognized, ironically, that for the European traveler, the phantasm of the private (sacred?) harem could be realized only within the public (profane?) world of the bordello.

Hence the breakdown of orientalist eroticism and its dispersion in a frustrated pornography that dispossesses it of its difference and multiplies the signs of banality within the space created by the very absence of the desired object: "Back in Benisouef, we had it off once [tiré un coup] (just like in Siout) in a hut so low-roofed that it was necessary to crawl in order to enter it" (Lettres, 239); "in Esneh, I had it off five times [tiré cinq coups] and licked cunt three times [gamahuché trois fois]. I say this without beating about the bush nor circumlocution" (Lettres, 242). Here, the orientalist's sexual exploits point to nothing beyond the emptiness of their signifiers of excess, which eradicate any possibility of climactic stylization. What is at stake here is not the desire for eroticism but the expression of a will to virility at a time of impotence.

Flaubert pushed the phantasm of Oriental eroticism to its limits so that he could confront the immanent lack that regulated it, encounter the familiar traces that it excluded, and experience the symbolic violence that it unleashed.

Melancholia

"[The] melancholies of the voyage," says Flaubert (symbolically, in his last letter from Egypt to Louis Bouilhet), "are perhaps one of the most beneficial aspects of traveling [une des choses les plus profitables des voyages]" (Lettres, 292). How could the orientalist traveler benefit from his melancholia, the extreme depression that he experienced throughout the journey and yet could not communicate? Leaving Egypt made Flaubert feel particularly melancholy because he could more distinctly experience his sense of loss: "It is always sad to leave a place when one knows one will never return," explains Flaubert just before considering his melancholia beneficial. Flaubert's depression was a kind of longing for the lost Other: Egypt, the symbolic representation of the place of nonreturnability.

For Flaubert, the Orient was the locus of melancholia. From the very moment he arrived, he encountered the "soleil noir": "A solemn and disturbing impression when I feel my feet pushing against the Egyptian soil" (Notes, 451). The "real Orient" constantly provides the belated traveler with "a dormant and melancholic effect . . . something immense and merciless in the middle of which you are lost" (Notes, 455). The melancholy traveler loses himself in the Orient and then mourns his loss. What distinguishes his relation to the Other from that of the optimistic orientalist—Maxime Du Camp, for example—is the experience of melancholic withdrawal and its articulation as unspecifiable loss. The Orient of the belated traveler is the merciless locus of shattered dreams and disillusionment; it exposes the retentive traveler to the absence of the object and robs/rubs him of his affective cohesion, of his joyful hope.

Although Flaubert was somewhat conscious of being deprived of the lost object, he disavowed his disbelief in the object and thus kept searching for it in metonymic objects of desire such as the mother or home and the Orient or the Other. The melancholy traveler is fixated on an anality that prevents him from separating himself from the object. Since there was no possibility of reconciliation with these displaced objects, Flaubert repeated his experience of loss in a chain of metonymic signification which rendered him even more morose—his desire to collect, we can see now, was an attempt to cope with his melancholia. Leaving, for Flaubert, meant the (re)experience of the loss and the recognition of the absence of the object. This was true of leaving both home and the Orient.[16]

Is the benefit of the journey's melancholia anything other than the noncommunicable grief of losing the object of desire itself? But what is the lost object? To speak of the lost object is to acknowledge its loss. The object is the unspecifiable, the unnamable, the unrepresented, because it exceeds the symbolic.[17] This is the reason for the melancholy traveler's inability to locate the object and speak of it. Flaubert did not know, nor could he communicate, what depressed him: "A cold and misty morning—atrociously sad until Choubra; it is impossible for me to talk" (*Notes*, 473); "sadness upon leaving the tombstones [of Karnac], why?" (*Notes*, 535). "Why am I so somber?" the traveler keeps asking himself, unable to explain anything to anyone, including himself.

The melancholia of travel is therefore about communicational failure: one can speak of it only by remaining silent. The perception of the Orient as the locus of melancholia creates a void in the belated traveler, impairs his intelligence, and empties him of his desire for representation; for example, "I must inform you quite seriously that my intelligence has greatly declined. It worries me, I am not joking the least. I feel very empty, very flat, very sterile. . . . What will I write? and even will I write?" (*Lettres*, 236). The sense of dejection and loss of interest impose on the belated orientalist a lack of meaning and a state of noncommunicability, thus compelling him or her to silence and discursive renunciation. The meaning of *mélancolie du voyage* is the loss of meaning in melancholia.

And yet, there is no tolerance for bereavement and loss in the symbolic field of orientalist discourse. Orientalism begins with the negation of loss, with a will to discovery. Endowed with the desire for and a power of representation, the orientalist is a sense maker, a creator of meaning; to discover and to represent the Other he must negate the experience of lack and his sense of disorientation.

The melancholy traveler, on the contrary, is the site of schizoid splitting: he acknowledges the loss and then tries to represent the asymbolia through the symbolic field of orientalist discourse: an impossible task. The belated orientalist does not know that the melancholic object interrupts the symbolic and exceeds it; he cannot recognize that he is a *stranger* in the familiar field of orientalist discourse; he is, in short, blind to his cognitive blankness, to his asymbolic condition, and to his semantic alienation.

The belated traveler is also ignorant and unconcerned about the implications of his melancholia. He does not know that the discovery of the loss of orientalist meaning is itself perhaps a new kind of meaning, that his silence has a potential for opposition to the semantic production in the orientalist field of knowledge. The belated traveler is an unconscious rebel without a cause, for he does not recognize that his gloomy noncommunicability is an unwitting rejection of the optimistic orientalist sense making, and thus the producer of a new knowledge. Was not Flaubert's despair a new kind of hyperlucidity? Did not his melancholia create a *beneficial* separation from the symbolic domain of orientalist representation?

The Figuration of Orientalist Discontents

Flaubert's Oriental journey was a failure. He went to Egypt in search of a visionary alternative, an *Other* discourse, and a "new" mode of representation that would have liberated him from the banalities of the mid-nineteenth-century discourses of power. Instead he encountered the absence of an "outside" view and realized the unattainability of a break with the dominant discourses and the impossibility of an alternative mode of representation. Such a failure is at once a symptom and a transgression of the discursive situation he wished to transcend. It is symptomatic because Flaubert's failure reaffirms that discourses of power, such as Orientalism, impose their epistemological and representational limits on any discursive practice that defines itself in a relation of opposition to them, thus impeding the possibility of articulating an *Other* discourse. Flaubert's belated Orientalism therefore unwittingly reproduced the very protocols of the discourse it wanted to exclude.

But such a reproduction of the dominant discourse comes with the voice of its discontents. Flaubert's explicit disillusionment with his Oriental project inscribed itself in orientalist discourse as an irreducible opposite that marked the very limits of Orientalism: the limit of its representation by exposing its clichés; the limit of its language by speaking its obscenities; the limit of its consciousness by acting out its unconscious perversities. Flaubertian transgression, therefore, is not the heroic triumph over the limit; nor is it the reactionary negation of the discursive boundary that surrounds it. It is, rather, the affirmation of the limit to the point where it exposes Orientalism's excess, discloses its repressions, and betrays its law.

Flaubert: the figuration of orientalist discontents.

4. Kipling's "Other" Narrator/Reader: Self-Exoticism and the Micropolitics of Colonial Ambivalence

✦

The 1987 Oxford edition of Rudyard Kipling's Anglo-Indian short stories (Life's Handicap, The Day's Work, The Man Who Would Be King, and Plain Tales from the Hills) is illustrated with what one might call "colonialist" photographs, which, like the author's fiction, depict different aspects of English life in India at the height of British rule. In the center of the cover photograph for The Day's Work, for example, a British writer (or a colonial administrator, perhaps) is sitting at a desk covered with books and papers, scribbling something, while looking straight into the camera's eye. He is flanked by two barefoot bearers dressed in white livery and accompanied by two other less elaborately dressed Indian servants (or just natives), who seem to be providing the master with some information from a native document. Similarly, the cover photograph of The Man Who Would Be King portrays a British lady in a rickshaw drawn by two coolies and accompanied by her dog and a third servant, who is pushing or standing guard behind the carriage. And, finally, the photograph on the cover of Plain Tales from the Hills shows a group of British men and women, presumably at the Simla Club, sitting outside at a table surrounded by bearers and servers (figure 6).

These photographs interest me, the postcolonial viewer, as a starting point for reading Kipling because their studium mobilizes a vague desire to understand and enjoy the otherwise undesirable scenes of the British Empire in the stories that follow.[1] They make me identify a field of cultural interest by allowing me to construct an imaginary world of images that corresponds to the historically "real" world of the empire as represented in Kipling's stories: the photograph of a woman riding in a rickshaw, for example, helps me envision the witty Mrs. Hauksbee, or even her ac-

knowledged original, Mrs. Burton, riding around Simla to meet a lover such as Mr. Bremmil, or perhaps on her way to rescue a callow subaltern like Pluffles from the hands of her rival, Mrs. Reiver. The cover photograph from *The Day's Work* makes me think of the scene of "white" writing and picture the mute, but so centrally present, writer of the dramatic monologues delivered by Oriental storytellers just on the periphery of his writing desk. I view these photographs as a testimony to the reality of the empire and enjoy them as historical scenes that evoke an unadorned sense of political commitment in me to read Kipling and to understand his place in the machinery of the colonial power.

Yet, beyond such simple, perhaps even naive, pleasures of identification, I have chosen to study these photographs as a means of broaching Kipling's Anglo-Indian fiction because they also delineate the complex outline of a split structure of mediation between the European subject of colonialism and the Oriental encountered in Kipling's stories of the empire.[2] On the one hand, these photographs depict, perhaps intentionally, the master-slave dialectic between the British colonizers and their Indian servants. In such a relation, the master's desire for recognition, and therefore power, is mediated through the presence of the slaves, whose marginal positions in the photographs highlight the British dominators. The slave's gratification must be refused so that the master's desire can be realized. The bare feet of the natives, their retracted gazes, and their submissive gestures—in contrast with the master, who is shod and looks straight at the camera, expressing his self-confidence—are all differential

Figure 6. Photos from the covers of the Oxford World Classics edition of three Kipling works: *The Day's Work*, ed. Thomas Pinney (Oxford: Oxford University Press, 1987), reproduced by permission of the British in India Museum; *The Man Who Would Be King*, ed. Louis L. Cornell (Oxford: Oxford University Press, 1987), reproduced by permission of Christie's Fine Art Auctioneers; *Plain Tales from the Hills*, ed. Andrew Rutherford (Oxford: Oxford University Press, 1987), reproduced by permission of the Trustees of the Bowood Collection.

signs of otherness that construct the identity of the colonizer. The photographs, then, reaffirm the fact that the production of colonial authority is dependent on the ever-present Other on the margins.

On the other hand, these photographs give figural representation to an unconscious *desire for self-exoticism* on the part of the colonizer that crosses the coded message of the pictures' *studium*. The desire for self-exoticism, as I will discuss shortly, consists of both a mimetic mode of identification with the exotic Other (i.e., "Thou art that") and a differential or negative mode of identification (i.e., "I am not the Other"—the Other being the "not-I"). The marginalized natives as photographic props mediate the colonizers' identity as "exotic"—the British colonizers wanting to look "different" from the British back home in England—while the colonizer's pensive gaze conveys an unexpected, even violent, flash of uncertainty that undermines his or her self-assured, confident pose. In these split photographs the master's desire for self-exoticism mediates for me, the postcolonial viewer, the retracted gaze of the natives, their repressed desires, their marginalized identity, and their unspoken words. When I look at these photographs, what I encounter is not so much the coded message of their *studium* but their *punctum* as a kind of subtle *beyond*, something that slips past the intentionality of the colonialist photographer and the photographed natives. From the perspective of the *punctum*, these photographic representations of the empire are not merely the expression of a unary colonialist message; they are the site of a split, an uncertainty, that exposes the return of the repressed and the desire for articulating the unspoken. What fills the sight of the postcolonial viewer, then, is the sense of a disturbing vacillation between the desire for masterly self-recognition—a kind of *méconnaissance*—and the desire for recognizing the Other, between controlling the native on the margins and allowing the expression of the uncontrollable, and, finally, between the monolithic articulation of imperial power and the deflecting utterance of its disturbing effects.

Such ideological ambivalences as the effects of a split structure of mediation between the colonizer and the colonized are at the heart of Kipling's representational practice. Traditionally, criticism of Kipling has repeatedly claimed his Anglo-Indian fiction to be a self-assured, direct representation of British imperialism. Whether on the right or on the left, Kipling's critics view his stories as the monolithic, official discourse of the empire, without any consideration of the possibility of heteroglossia and discursive gaps as moments of uncertainty in Kipling's narratives.[3] To read Kipling's fiction merely as an unmediated picture of late nineteenth-century Anglo-India by "the prophet of British Imperialism in its expansionist phase . . . and also the unofficial historian of the British army" is not only to dismiss a substantial part of his stories—the gaps, the lapses, the unspoken words—but to fall back into a pre-Bakhtinian mode of criticism that views "realist" fiction as a pure and monologic representation of the real.[4]

I propose, on the contrary, a reading of the colonialist text that takes into account the possibility of a split between the manifest text, which is the scene of "white" authorial writing (the agency of knowing at work), and the "unconscious" discourse as the site where the unspoken and the unspeakable surface in the manifest text through the speaking subject's lapses and uncertainties (the meaning here being produced through [re]reading and interpreting Kipling's text by a "belated" postcolonial reader). Reading Kipling's stories as the site of a split mediation involves a kind of perforating or cutting of the text to explode the plurality of its messages, because such a text is itself marked by a plurality of subject positions as opposed to monologic authorial narration (or official discourse). As in the case of the colonial photographs, what I read in Kipling is not always the intentional, coded message of the stories but the subtle beyond, the "sliding signifiers" that escape the text's intentionality and expose its uncertainties, splits, and ambivalences—ambivalences and splits that are ideologically productive in enabling the discriminatory power of cultural colonialism to work. The colonial authority in Kipling is constructed precisely through the mediated function of the unconscious discourse and its effects of splitting.[5]

Not surprisingly, my reading of the split in Kipling is itself split. First, on a thematic level, I am concerned with the micropolitical effects of the mediated relation of the colonizer to the native: To what extent does the native become the mediator of the colonizer's desire for recognition? How is the colonizer's experience of the Other articulated in the manifest text as "alienation"? Second, on a narrative level, I am interested in how the scene of white writing incorporates the native, thus producing another structure of mediation in which the uncertainties and ambivalences of the colonialist writer become the mediating signs of the unspoken and the unspeakable, whose effects are reimplicated in the relations of colonial power. Is the desire to represent the Other itself a mediator for the possible realization of the unrepresented? What are the ideological effects and implications of the return of the repressed?

Colonial Alienation

Before I begin discussing the thematic issue of the colonizer's relation to the Other, I must explain my use of the term *alienation*. Is my use of the term a Marxist one that signifies the process through which a group of people (the proletariat) become alienated from the products of their own activity, and with respect to the status of their existence? Or is it a Lacanian usage, which sees the structure of alienation as that of a *vel* with a "dissymmetric" relation between the subject and the Other?[6] It may be both and/or neither. I speak of three kinds of alienation in Kipling's work. First, there is the colonizer's inability to see the implications of his or her colonial involvement and situation in India. Kipling's colonial figures often remain apart from what they actually *do* in India, and from what they produce in the empire's machinery of power. Second, there is the cultural alienation that I call "self-exoticism." The British colonizers spent long periods, sometimes their entire lives, in India, and so they often felt alienated from "home" (and in that sense inclined to identify themselves as "Indians") while simultaneously remaining alienated (as "English") with respect to the Indians as "natives." Third, I am speaking of a psychological problem of identifying oneself through a misrecognition (méconnaissance) of the native as the Other. Here the alienation renders the relation of the colonialist subject to the colonized object (objectified?) a kind of narcissistic self-acknowledgment: the colonizer misidentifies himself or herself in the mirror presence of the Other and is thus alien to his or her own subjectivity. Finally, I also use alienation to imply Kipling's own situation with respect to his discursive practice and to the ideological ambivalences of the colonial texts he produced.

Home and the Colony: The Experience of the Uncanny

Central to the production of the colonizer's desire for self-exoticism—that is, the site of a split between the mimetic identification with the Oriental and the differential construction of identity through a disavowal of the Other's subjectivity—is his or her experience of the uncanny (Unheimlich), for exoticism presupposes an unfamiliar, unhomelike setting posited against the peaceful security of home. It is for this reason that the field of the Other is often thematized in colonial fiction as the site of the uncanny surrounded by images of foreignness, fear, and horror. Such a frightful encounter with the Other finds its most striking expression in one of Kipling's sketches, "The City of Dreadful Night" (1891).[7] This short sketch describes the narrator's nocturnal ramble through the squalid streets of Lahore, ending with the scene of a woman's corpse being carried to the Moslem burial ground.

As an account of the narrator's nightmarish experience, the sketch replicates every category of the uncanny he encounters. First, a dreadful sense of claustrophobia is conveyed through the description of "the dense wet heat that hung over the city, like a blanket."[8] Restless in his dark and empty room, the narrator sets out for a stroll in the streets but encounters the uncanny vision of a dead city, exhausted by the stifling heat and invaded by "yelling jackals" and vagrant dogs. Walking in the city proves to be no less eerie than staying in the solitary room, for it too is dark, silent, and deadly. "The long line of the naked dead," the "stifling hot blast from the mouth of Delhi Gate," and "the stifling silence [that] settles down over the City of Dreadful Night" make Lahore resemble a giant graveyard (LH, 271, 275). The feeling of the uncanny is intensified by a compulsive return to the same horrific scene: "More corpses ... and again more corpses" (LH, 271). The field of the Other, then, becomes an inescapable prison where every turn away from the uncanny brings the subject back to it.

Read as the manifest text, the images of the uncanny in "The City of Dreadful Night" are consistent with the orientalist stereotypes of the Other: India is portrayed as a primitive, dark, and enigmatic domain devoid of the energy and rigor of a European city, and the Orientals are literally equated with "sheeted corpses," lacking all initiative or desire for change. The negative vision of the Oriental is important to the colonizer's identity because it provides him with an "imaginary" Other onto whom his anxieties and fears are projected. The striking contrast between the restless narrator, who is stimulated by the heat to stroll and write, and the heat-stricken natives, reduced to motionless bodies, pinpoints the colonizer's differential mode of identification. In the context of the colonized's total negation—the sheeted corpses being denied any subjectivity—the colonizer's desire is no longer a desire for recognition by a conscious Other but a narcissistic self-acknowledgment in the frightful mirror. Here the Other is no longer the subject's alter ego but merely a differential signifier, a medium that produces meaning only for the colonialist subject. The manifest text of the colonizer thus excludes the Other from its semantic field in its very gesture of inclusion: the Other is the locus of nonmeaning, of "stifling silence," of death and profound darkness.

And yet, if the uncanny is the return of something familiar and established that is transformed by repression into morbid anxiety, the colonizer's narcissistic self-recognition must be viewed also as the expression of his own alienation. In the middle of the sketch, the narrator says of the dreadful spectacle that "Doré might have drawn it! Zola could describe it" (LH, 273). In the light of these statements and the title's intertextual reference to James Thompson's poem, "The City of Dreadful Night" appears as a familiar projection of an earlier sense of disorientation as expressed in Doré's grotesque and dark drawings of London and in Zola's gloomy representations of Paris. Even though he is conscious of his sketch's intertexts, the colonialist narrator (an alienated subject of discourse) does not see their relation to his own discursive production—that is, the effects of mediation projected into the European intertexts that negate his own colonialist vision of the Other as mimetically produced earlier, at "home."

He fails to realize that the sketch represents not an alien city, as he seems to think, but the familiar scene of an alienating European city. In this sense, the representation of horror is itself symptomatic of a horror of re-presenting (reencountering) the earlier sense of alienation.

The colonizer's symptomatic projection of his morbid anxieties and fears onto the Other perpetuates his sense of alienation because such an exteriorization distances him further from the internal predicament of self-identification. In his imaginary (specular?) mode of identification, the colonizer projects his earlier (primordial) sense of loss onto the Other and essentializes his fixation as a "natural" or "real" phenomenon. Instead of recognizing the Other's subjectivity, he objectifies the Other as the source of all his morbid anxieties and fears—the natives in "The City of Dreadful Night" become the incarnation of the colonizer's terror of death, and India appears as the quintessence of his fears of silence, darkness, and solitude.

Colonialist Nostalgia

One of the effects produced when the colonizer projects his anxieties onto the Other is a regressive longing for home. This is exemplified by Private Ortheris, who, while drinking beer with the narrator, feels "sick for London again; sick for the sounds of 'er, an the sights of 'er, and the stinks of 'er; orange-peel and hasphalte an' gas comin' in over Vaux'all Bridge" (PTH, 210). The soldier's experience in India exposes a yearning, a lack, as he compares his present state of nonsatisfaction with the fantasy of a previous state of satisfaction at home. Ortheris describes his pleasant memories of London as a counterprojection of his anxieties in India: he is sick for the "sights" and "sounds" of London, just the opposites—though similar in their negativity—of the darkness and silence he has encountered in India. In this sense, Ortheris's homesickness reinforces his sense of alienation because it generates an ideal image that is in fact a counterprojection of the lack he has experienced in the field of the Other.

The treatment of Ortheris's "madness" by Mulvaney and the narrator-reporter confirms the impossibility of recovering the lost object (the mother city/culture), which brings the colonizer to accept his alienated situation as a "Tommy—a bloomin', eight-anna, dog-stealin' Tommy, with a number instead of a decent name" in India (PTH, 208). When Mulvaney's attempt to treat Ortheris's madness through physical coercion fails, the narrator suggests a new cure by offering to exchange his civilian clothes with the soldier's uniform and to give him money to help him desert the army—what one may call a *disciplinary* cure of alienation. But when the narrator and Mulvaney return to the scene, having abandoned him for awhile, Ortheris has shaken off his "mad" impulse to desert the army: "The devils had departed from Private Stanley Ortheris, No. 22639, B Company. The loneliness, the dusk, and the waiting had driven them out as I had hoped" (PTH, 213). The experience of darkness and solitude in civilian clothes helps Ortheris discover the absence of the lost object of desire. Ironically, however, the symbolic journey to London through the mediation of civilian clothes makes the soldier accept his alienated identity as "Private Ortheris, No. 22639, B Company." The loss of home leaves the common soldier with only one option—becoming an "insignificant" member of the authoritarian organization of the imperial army. Ortheris's return to his own clothes when he discovers the futility of his fantasy is a symbolic return to the alienated space of the colonial army. The irony of the narrator's statement is a duplicitous reaffirmation of the soldier's identity as a number: the discipline works through the mediation of its effects of delinquency—for example, the ghettoized colonial soldier, the alienated reporter.

Demand for Love, or a Metonymy for Home

But if London and all its images of comfort are lost due to colonial displacement, what can the average colonizer do in India to overcome his morbid anxieties? To turn the site of the uncanny into a comfortable home, some colonizers try to recuperate the most obvious metaphor for the lost object of desire: the mother's affection and love.[9] A young officer's self-delusionary love for a British woman is a recurrent theme in the *Plain Tales from the Hills*. Interestingly, Kipling's fiction contextualizes the demand for love by elaborating on the colonizer's alienating situation in the machinery of the imperial power. In India, the colonizers are either exiled to a "jungle" or an "out-district, with nobody to talk to and a great deal of work to do" (PTH, "In Error," 133), or confined to an office where they are made "to think that there is nothing but their work, and nothing like their work" (PTH, "Wressley of the Foreign Office," 224). Therefore, when a civil engineer like Moriarty comes "fresh out of the jungle to a big city," or, say, a Foreign Service officer like Wressley wanders in the streets "between office and office," he is "overwhelmed . . . knocked . . . down, and left . . . gasping as though he had been a little schoolboy" by the first British woman he encounters (PTH, 226).

Yet, ironically, love does not cure his sense of alienation. Instead it becomes only another form of social subjection—he becomes the slave of the British mistress. The infatuation of Pluffles, a newly arrived sub-altern, with the "cold and hard" Mrs. Reiver is a case in point:

> He learned to fetch and carry like a dog, and to wait like one, too, for a word from Mrs. Reiver. He learned to keep appointments which Mrs. Reiver had no intention of keeping. He learned to take thank-fully dances which Mrs. Reiver had no intention of giving him. He learned to shiver for an hour and a quarter on the windward side of Elysium while Mrs. Reiver was making up her mind to come for a ride. He learned to hunt for a 'rickshaw, in a light dress-suit under pelting rain and to walk by the side of that 'rickshaw when he had found it. He learned what it was to be like a coolie and ordered about like a cook. (PTH, "The Rescue of Pluffles," 44)

Whereas in relation to the natives the colonizer may appear as a powerful master, the demand for love turns him into a slave. "Bound hand and foot to Mrs. Reiver's 'rickshaw wheels," Pluffles is literally another of her coolies, a situation that extends his virtual enslavement as a subordinate officer in the service of the imperial army to his private life, and as such consolidates his alienation.[10] Needless to say, the demand for love always leads to disillusionment because the colonialist subject who does not take into account the woman's subjectivity demands something from her that she cannot give. Every love story in the *Plain Tales from the Hills* ends with the man feeling "broken, smashed" by the woman who refuses to reciprocate his love (PTH, 228). As a result, the demand for love is always a lesson in frustration and humiliation; the search for the lost object, love, always ends in the discovery of its absence.

Desire for the Other, or Erotic Domination

While some colonizers try to master their morbid anxieties through amo-rous affairs with British women, others are tempted to embrace their phobia by immersing themselves in—or, more appropriately, "penetrat-ing"—the Other. A familiar figure in Kipling's Anglo-Indian fiction is the colonizer who goes native—"going Fantee," as it was termed by the British (PTH, 24). Manifestations of the exposure to native life vary from a superficial orientalist masquerade, as in the case of detective Strickland, who gets pleasure from wearing Indian costumes and imitating "Oriental culture,"[11] to a more profound search for knowledge by a converted colonizer, Jellaludin McIntosh in "To Be Filed for Reference." But the desire for immersion is most commonly manifested in the form of an erotic relation with a native woman. "Beyond the Pale," "Georgie Poorgie," and "Without the Benefit of the Clergy" are all variations on this familiar theme. What draws the British protagonists of these stories "beyond the pale" of their genteel society and "deep away in the heart of the city" is a transgressive search for the "oriental passion and impulsiveness," which they have read about in "the old *Arabian Nights*" (PTH, 127, 131). In contrast to the sexually inhibited women of the club, the native woman is represented as a sexualized figure incapable of resisting her master's desire; the racial difference makes her powerless.

As a fantasy of erotic domination, the sexual relation with the native woman appeals to the colonizer's imagination because it combines erotic desire with the desire for mastery. Indeed, in every instance, the British protagonist is gratified not only by "endless delight" and "strange things" that happen during the night but by the woman's acknowledgment of his mastery and dominance (PTH, 129, 130). In "Without the Benefit of the Clergy," to give an example, Ameera constantly reminds John Holden that "I know that I am thy servant and thy slave and the dust under thy feet" (LH, 125). The subordination of Ameera makes Holden a "king in his own territory," "the lord of the house," allowing him thus to create a little colony of his own (LH, 116, 119).

Although the erotic domination of the native woman by the male colonizer seems ideologically consistent with the colonialist mentality, the woman's "low caste" renders such a relationship "an inconsistent affair" (LH, 116). Kipling's moralistic narrator always reminds the reader that "a man should, whatever happens, keep to his own caste, race, and breed. Let the White go to the White and the Black to the Black" (PTH, 127). Kipling thus reaffirms the hierarchical structure of the colonialist ideology of race. Since colonial authority depends on racial differentiation, this crossing of racial boundaries is considered an act of transgression. As a result, the colonizer's affair with the native woman forces him to live a "double life." Christopher Trejago's situation in "Beyond the Pale" provides an example of this cultural predicament: "In the day-time, Trejago drove through his routine of office work, or put on his calling-clothes and called on the ladies of the Station, wondering how long they would know him if they knew of poor Bisesa. At night, when all the City was still, came the walk under the evil-smelling boorka, the patrol through Jitha Megji's bustee, the quick turn into Amir Nath's Gully between the sleeping cattle and the dead walls, and then, last of all, Bisesa, and the deep, even breathing of the old woman who slept outside the door of the bare little room that Durga Charon allotted to his sister's daughter" (PTH, 130). The contrasting images of day and night, life and death, order and labyrinthine disorder point to the split in the colonizer's identity. The office and colonial station are identified as the domain of social obligation, respectability, and consciousness; the dead walls and dark room of Bisesa mark the scene of desire, transgression, and the unconscious. Trejago's act of satisfying his transgressive desire for the native woman, intertwined with his desire for mastery, inscribes a gap in his identity and produces the effect of dividing him between the conscious agent of colonial power and the unconscious subject of a defiant attempt to cross its racial boundaries.

Trejago's predicament is paradigmatic of the contradictions inherent in the colonial identity of Kipling's characters. Inscribed within the economies of desire *and* domination, the colonizer's relation to the Other depends on both recognition and disavowal of the native's subjectivity. The colonizer's narcissistic mode of self-acknowledgment (self-exoticism), mediated through the objectified (or appropriated) presence of the native, produces a split in the colonial identity, the site of both desire and power. To put it a bit differently, the desire for domination entails and has a place for both identification and alienation, fear and desire. Behind the subject's manifest intention to exercise his colonial power are his terrifying sense of alienation and his latent desire to recognize, even identify with, the native, for the Other is, after all, the locus of dreams, fantasies, and desires that are repressed by the colonizer's culture. Here, both the transgressive desire for the native woman and the desire for the colonial power reproduce each other as their effects in a spiral relation that engenders only alienation and discontent.

The Other Storyteller: Narrative Self-Exoticism

The uncertainties and ambivalences of colonial identity are not only thematic problems in Kipling's fiction, they are also embedded and replicated in the micropolitics of narrative economy as parts of the writer's own representational practice. As a colonialist writer, Kipling was inscribed within the same structure of alienating identification as his fictional characters. His narrative therefore is the site of a split between the manifest text of an authorial writing and the excluded discourse that surfaces in the manifest text as noise, as a disturbing figure of its unconscious. I will broach the issue of narrative-textual split—the split between the scene of white authorial writing and the unconscious and repressed expression of the Other's discourse figured as noise—in two ways: first, I consider briefly the general problem of narrative framing as an ambivalent technique; second, I concentrate more specifically on the micropolitics of Kipling's representational practice as the site of an ontological split between writing and speaking.

Framing, as narrative theory has demonstrated, is by definition a device for splitting the narrative economy, for positing at least two positions for the speaking subject. The most obvious narrative ambivalence in Kipling is his use of framing technique. Kipling's narrators are often strange renditions of the duplicitous relation between colonial writer and colonialist-orientalist discourse: while some narrators in his stories are hysterically authoritarian, authoritative, and world-weary colonial experts, some of his "Other" storytellers are disempowered, disenfranchised, and marginalized natives. The inclusion of Orientals as storytellers or speakers of dramatic monologues addressed to sahibs, I suggest, expresses a narrative desire for the Other—a desire that "dialogizes" the monolithic (authorial) discourse—while it simultaneously points to a hegemonic impulse to appropriate the native voice. To be sure, to adopt a native narrator is an act of discursive appropriation because the colonialist writer takes advantage of a "voice" that does not belong to him. The dramatic monologues of the natives are never "authentic" representations of Oriental culture; they are narrative masquerades reminiscent of detective Strickland's orientalist disguises. The stories are usually a series of detached, fragmentary pieces extracted from the "exotic" scene surrounding the colonialist writer, who has little interest in fully understanding or representing the native's condition. The Oriental storyteller, often reduced to a rhetorical or narrative device, is thus appropriated by the colonialist writer to provide an exotic flavor for his familiar tale while showing his mastery in imitating the Other's speech. In this sense, the inclusion of the native as a narrative frame reaffirms his exteriority in relation to the story's actual interlocutionary situation, which is that of "white" writing for "white" readers. It is not fortuitous that the narratees in all the dramatic monologues turn out to be sahibs whose silent presence is constantly acknowledged by the Oriental narrators. As self-situating devices, the references to the master's presence define the status of the reader as that of a white colonizer and thus exclude the natives from the stories' system of communication. In short, the natives are excluded mediators of a white-to-white relation: inclusion is a figure for exclusion here.

And yet, the incorporation of the native speaker into the colonialist text can be also viewed as an instance of what Bakhtin calls heteroglossia. Even though the Other's story serves to express the colonialist writer's own interests and intentions, it nonetheless refracts his monolithic discourse because, as Bakhtin argues, "the speech of such narrators is always *another's speech* (as regards the real or potential direct discourse of the author) and in *another's language* (i.e., insofar as it is a particular variant of the literary language that clashes with the language of the narrator)."[12] To posit a native storyteller as the speaking subject inevitably implies the inclusion of a linguistic—and by extension ideological—system that is different from the writer's own system. The Other's monologue splits or dialogizes the colonial writer's discourse as another point of view, another voice; it subtly insinuates itself into his text. This is not to claim that the Other can or does talk back in the colonialist text—the native is always in this structure the excluded third between the colonial writer and his British readers—but the objectified presence of the Oriental storyteller introduces an "internal bifurcation," to borrow Bakhtin's words again, that undermines the unitary language and monologic style of the colonialist text and makes it an example of discursive self-exoticism—the colonialist text here being attracted to the Other's identity, against which it is defining itself. As I will discuss shortly, Kipling's text depends for its narrative economy on the "excluded" presence of the native as a dialogizing background, or as noise, a kind of elusive resonance that haunts and disturbs the authoritative discourse while mediating the productivity of its colonial authority.

One may sense traces of such elusive voices in "Gemini," for example, in which a native begins and ends his story with a critique of the British judicial system in India. Showing his mutilated body to the sahib as evidence, Durga Dass complains that "there is no justice in courts."[13] The victim of mistaken identity, he appropriately identifies the judicial system as inefficient and lacking all regard for the oppressed. Recognizing the power of written statements, the native speaker, who is initially excluded from the scene of white writing, convinces the sahib at the end to "take a pen and write clearly what [he has] said, that the Dipty Sahib may see, and reprove the Stunt Sahib" (B&W, 231). Similarly, in "At Howli Thana," the native narrator frames his mendacious self-vindication with a brief description of poverty among the natives as he convincingly explains how his "three little children whose stomachs are always empty" will die unless he is employed by the distrustful sahib to whom he addresses the elaborate tale of his dismissal from the police force (B&W, 205). Here too the native is able to convince the sahib to employ him and recognize his

resourcefulness. Beyond such thematic effects of double-voiced narration, the use of Oriental storytellers is important to Kipling's text for its
theoretical implications in the context of the writer's own representational practice. Here the role of Oriental storyteller exposes the ideological difference between the art of colonial fiction and the native's oral tradition. Let me explain this issue with the specific example of Kipling's
preface to Life's Handicap (1890). To contextualize his book for the reader,
Kipling recounts his (imaginary?) encounter with Gobind, a one-eyed
wandering mendicant living his last few days of life in the Chubara of
Dhunni Bhagat, a monastery in northern India. The first conversation with
the holy man, who turns out to have been "once a famed teller of stories
when [he] was begging on the road between Koshin and Etra," inspires
Kipling to write the book (LH, 6–7). Gobind's stories, told "in a voice like
the rumbling of heavy guns over a wooden Bridge," mediate Kipling's
relation to his own text (LH, 6). The identity of the colonial writer is thus
produced differentially through the mirror presence of the Oriental storyteller, whose function is that of an alter ego (an Other). Kipling describes
to Gobind his profession as "a Kerani—one who writes with a pen upon
paper not being in the service of the Government"—and explains the
economic aspect of his practice by pointing out that "the tales are sold
and money accrues to me that I may keep alive" (LH, 6). In response,
Gobind compares the writer's practice with that of the bazaar storyteller:
"That is the work of the bazar story-teller; but he speaks straight to men
and women and does not write anything at all. Only when the tale has
aroused expectation, and calamities are about to befall the virtuous, he
stops suddenly and demands payment ere he continues the narration"
(LH, 6). On the surface, the colonial writer views himself as the modern
version of the traditional storyteller. The art of colonial fiction sees itself in
the "mirror" of the Other's oral tradition and says, "There I am." Like the
bazaar storyteller, Kipling participates in the political and economical systems of his community from the marginal position he occupies—the
position of "not being in the service of the Government." But the empire's
storyteller quickly distinguishes his art from that of the bazaar storyteller
by reaffirming the difference between writing and speech. Whereas Gobind's tales belong to the ephemeral domain of speech, Kipling's stories
mark the domain of monumental writing. Here the colonial artist identifies himself by saying, "I am not the Other"—the negative containing the
appropriation it seeks to negate.

The difference between writing and speech is important because it determines the power structure involved in the mediating relation between the colonialist writer and the Oriental storyteller. In the realm of colonial fiction, it is not speech that is privileged but writing. The native's speech is the external, the nontranscendental, against which Kipling defines his representational practice. Speech is also the inferior term that poses a kind of threat to the colonizer's writing. In introducing Gobind, Kipling notes that "his tales were true, but not one in twenty could be printed in an English book, because the English do not think as natives do" (LH, 6). The native's oral tales are the scene of a potentially disturbing unconscious that must be excluded in the conscious domain of monumental writing for it to produce the order of meaning, the "higher presence" that confers on the white writer the power of representation. Authority in the colonial text is thus the authorization to decide what must be written and what should be excluded.

Yet, as every exclusion implies the return of the excluded, the Other's speech insinuates itself into the conscious text of the colonizer by leaving the marks of its absence on the surface of the text. Kipling finishes the story of his encounter with Gobind by recounting a final conversation with him in which he promises the old storyteller to inscribe his name in the beginning of the book:

> "But it is a pity that our book is not born. How shall I know that there is any record of my name?"
>
> "Because I promise, in the forepart of the book, preceding everything else, that it shall be written, Gobind, sadhu, of the island in the river and awaiting God in Dhunni Bhagat's Chubara, first spoke of the book," said I. (LH, 8)

The presence of Gobind's name signifies the absence of his tales, the censure of his words in the sahib's text. Here the desire to include (represent) is the revelation of an absence, the sign of a void, the mark of what cannot be written and must be excluded. Kipling finishes his preface by acknowledging that "the most remarkable stories are, of course, those which do not appear—for obvious reasons" (LH, 9). The native's tales constitute an Other discourse that is outside the scene of white writing. Nonetheless, the native tale is beyond closure since it produces the elusive mark of its exclusion on the conscious text—that is the kind of rupture that forces Kipling to see the mediated structure of his fiction and recognize its mode of exclusion. The exclusion of the Other's stories and speech as the domain of the unconscious in white writing makes the beginning of Kipling's text ambivalent. As an alienated subject of colonial discourse, Kipling situates his text in a split between a kind of narcissistic self-identification mediated through the native's oral tradition and a differentiation from the Other's speech. The beginning of *In Black and White*—the title itself being suggestive of the split mode of representation in the practice of both native black and colonialist white—is literally divided between two kinds of situational self-reference. The book, on the one hand, begins with the writer's dedication, which is a pastiche of seventeenth-century dedicatory styles. Offering his third book to his "Moft Deare Father" as part of his "unpayable Debt" to such a great *Vstad* (or *Mafter*), Kipling acknowledges in an archaic, high-falutin' style his filial relation to the European tradition that has furnished him with the power of representation. The dedication confirms that the authority to represent also depends on the authorization derived from the symbolic father to whom the colonialist writer is indebted. Here, the structure of colonial desire to represent sustains the structure of the Law, which binds the colonialist writer to the written tradition. As a self-situating device, the pastiche then defines the context of the book and its addressee as European.

The dedication is followed, however, by an introduction written as a pastiche of the vernacular speech delivered by the writer's native servant, who wants to be honored for his task of putting the pages of the book together and for having taken care of the writer. On the first level of its colonial complicity, the orientalist pastiche is meant to be read as a kind of colonialist humor. Khadir Baksh's exaggerated demand to be recognized as a coauthor just for having put the pages in order makes him a comic figure whose ignorance is apt to reaffirm the (colonialist) reader's racial stereotypes of the natives.

The author's appropriation of his native servant as the speaker of his introduction to the stories is also intended to accentuate the demarcation of the writing scene as the sahib's privileged domain. Khadir Baksh begins his speech by reaffirming that the book was written by his master:

Hazur,—Through your favor this is a book written by my sahib. I know that he wrote it, because it was his custom to write far into the night; . . . it was my fate to sit without the door until the work was accomplished. Then came I and made shut all papers in the office-box, and these papers, by the peculiar operation of the Time and owing to the skillful manner in which I picked them up from the floor, became such a book as you now see. God alone knows what is written therein, for I am a poor man and the sahib is my father and mother, and I have no concern with the writing until he has left his table and gone to bed. (B&W, 161)

The scene of writing is white; the black presence of the native is excluded. Made to wait outside while the master is writing, Khadir Baksh can only be a witness to the product, never its active agent. As the servant of the white writer, the native enters the scene, symbolically, only when the action is ended and the work accomplished. The native's marginal presence and the appropriation of his speech as a kind of narrative self-exoticism serve the author's own narcissistic mode of identification: "I, the orientalist-colonialist writer, am the producer of the book." On the first level of signification, then, the function of white writing, like the colonialist project itself, is to appropriate the native and his speech and manufacture it as written stories for its English audience.

Yet, if the writer's use of situational self-reference is mediated through the Other, then the introduction can imply a second structure of meaning in which the ironic mode of identification can itself be ironized in the (postcolonial?) act of reading or interpreting. Indeed, it is ironic that the writer who wants to identify the context of his text as white chooses his native servant as the book's "gate-keeper," so to speak. The writer's intentional appropriation of the native speaker manifests a latent recognition of the servant's claim, which is originally repressed in the master's text, that wants to exclude the possibility of an Other meaning. In this sense, Khadir Baksh's misguided demand for honor can be read as an accurate and justified claim: not only does Khadir Baksh as the head of the sahib's household provide the master with the material necessary for his writing, but the native is also the one who supplies the white writer with the oral tales, or "raw material," which the latter manufactures as written stories of the empire for his own profit, thus reproducing discursively the empire's system of economic exploitation. Ironically, In Black and White acknowledges the crucial role of Khadir Baksh as the book's "gate-keeper" who introduces the reader to its Indian context, without which there would be no stories to tell.

The Productive Function of Colonial Ambivalence

The possibility of a second order of meaning is crucial to understanding the orientalist-colonialist discourse because it undermines the discourse's "polarities of intentionality."[14] The modern mode of colonial representation—the split discourse—in Kipling's fiction is neither a closed structure of meaning nor a coherent system of power, and consequently should not be treated as a homogeneous, orderly series of statements. Rather, it is a practice comprised of a complex system of irregular, disorderly utterances. The split in Kipling's representational practice articulates the censored discontinuities in the discourse of colonialist fiction, which as a discourse of power depends on producing an effect of order and unity—the order and unity it claims to have. The exclusion of the native from its discursive domain and the censoring of an Other meaning in its semantic field, on the one hand, inscribe a gap in the colonialist discourse in which the excluded third—the native and his voice at the margin—disturbs the certainty surrounding the writing subject. Although the text of the colonial writer is always mediated, as a discourse of power it represses the phenomenon of mediation because it demonstrates the "constructed" status of its meaning, particularly of the discursive subject. But the excluded mediator nevertheless returns to make "noise" in its communicational system or to haunt the discourse as a figure of its unconscious. Like the colonialist photograph, Kipling's text carries with it a subtle "beyond" that escapes the intentionality of its author. The colonialist writer, as an alienated subject of discourse, is never in full control of his representational practice. He is always leaving out or excluding something that traverses and "pricks" the smooth surface of the coded message.

In Kipling's fiction, both the gesture of exclusion and the return of the excluded are readable, which illustrates that the discourse of colonial power can be constituted only by means that deflect its coded message and produce "splits" in its apparent unity and confidence. The inclusion of the voice of the excluded native in Kipling is productive in that it engenders the split that displaces the site of racial differentiation inherent in the discriminatory mode of colonial power. The split in Kipling disturbs the mimetic mode of identification (self-exoticism), but its effects are reimplicated in the colonial authority, which works precisely through a kind of proliferation of difference—the exclusion in cultural colonialism works through the gesture of inclusion. In Kipling, colonial authority is exercised not through the silent repression of the excluded third—the native and his or her voice—but by the mediating effects of the split whereby it produces the "visible" difference that defines the discursive conditions of domination.

5. Colonial Ethnography and the Politics of Gender: The Everyday Life of an Orientalist Journey

✳

On August 13, 1850, in a letter to Théophile Gautier, Flaubert wrote from Jerusalem, "It is time to hurry. Before very long the Orient will no longer exist. We are perhaps the last of its contemplators."[1] This desperately urgent *invitation au voyage* expresses acutely the sense of belatedness late nineteenth-century orientalists felt toward the exotic Other in relation to earlier European travelers. Arriving too late to the Orient, at a time when tourism and European colonialism had already turned the exotic into the familiar, the belated traveler encountered the difficulty, if not the impossibility, of finding an elsewhere, of finding alternative horizons to explore, discover, and conquer. Late nineteenth-century orientalists thus faced the dilemma of how to become traveler-writers of the exotic in an age of colonial dissolution. Where did one go from there? Where could one find an "authentic Other"? For most French orientalists, as I argue in previous chapters, the condition of belatedness produced a melancholy discourse of nostalgia in which longing for the disappearing Other takes center stage and aporia displaces pseudoscientific certainty as the dominant rhetorical condition. Modern French travelers such as Nerval, Flaubert, Loti, and Eberhardt tried to represent the signifiers of the Other's absence as melancholic signs of an exotic presence on the verge of disappearing. Chris Bongie rightly compares this discourse to that of fetishism, in which the traveler takes as present what is already absent. Such a traveler undertakes a project that "cannot help coming after what it must come before."[2] The belated traveler thus transforms his or her experience of loss into a representation of the Orient as a site for melancholia and even mourning.

The somber discourse of nostalgia (for a time when "real" adventures were possible) is surprisingly absent from late nineteenth-century British travel writing. In contrast to the French orientalists' sense of loss and disorientation, belatedness produced in British travelers a peculiarly valiant desire to discover new places at a time when British colonialism had already expanded its power to all corners of the globe, leaving few places to discover and conquer. Far from the kind of "fatidic pessimism" Flaubert expresses in his letter to Gautier, British orientalists from Sir Richard Burton to T. E. Lawrence were driven by a positivistic urge to find an "elsewhere" still unexplored by previous travelers, a place where a traveler could still become a pioneer, a heroic adventurer, and have an "authentic" experience of otherness. It is precisely this search for an "unmarked" space that made the Arabian and African Sahara deserts appeal to the imagination of these Victorian travelers. The aura of "authentic" and dangerous exoticism associated with regions that remained "white blots" on European maps, to use Burton's words, provided British orientalists with alternative horizons to describe, measure, sketch, and make visible for their European audiences. Often couched as "pilgrimages," these ideological voyages were embedded in both a belated desire for otherness mediated by earlier accounts of the Orient and in a colonialist economy of information that enabled the very conditions of their possibility. Braced with a compelling ideology of adventure and supported by a powerful system of colonial relations, the belated traveler simultaneously pursued a fiercely individualistic adventure and acted as an ethnographer for the colonial system's information-gathering apparatus; their affiliations included the Royal Geographical Society, the Royal Asiatic Society, and the Foreign Office.

These belated voyages unfold a crucial moment in the history of Orientalism in which the solitary quest for elsewhere as a response to the onset of modernity in Europe becomes crucially productive in the micropolitics of imperial conquest. Turning against the homogenizing effects of "modern civilization" in an optimistic project of recovering, and perhaps eternalizing, the disappearing Other, the orientalist traveler undertakes an "experimentum crucis," to cite Burton's words again, which ironically produces the kind of epistemological visibility that would contribute to colonialism's hegemonic and homogenizing tendencies.

In this chapter I consider the microphysics of the complex relation between the belated traveler's desire for an elsewhere and the "geo-ethnography" of the Arabian Desert in an exemplary text, Lady Anne Blunt's *Pilgrimage to Nejd* (1881). An explorer, orientalist scholar, and strong supporter of Arab nationalism, Blunt traveled extensively throughout the

Middle East between 1875 and 1882 with her husband, Wilfrid Scawen Blunt. *Pilgrimage*, composed from Lady Anne's travel notes, is the account of their journey through the Nefud Desert to Nejd and then through the Euphrates Valley to Persia in search of information about "authentic" Bedouin culture and Arabian horses. At once a series of ethnographic field notes, geographical descriptions of the desert, and (auto)biographical accounts of the arduous journey, this plural text is actively situated between, on the one hand, a colonial system of meaning, and, on the other, a personal, individualistic interest in Bedouin culture which involved at times writing against Europeans' desire for domination in the Middle East—as, for example, in the Blunts' stance against the colonialist project of constructing a railway system in the Euphrates Valley and in strong support of Arab nationalism. But *Pilgrimage* is not merely an instance of "narrative-description duality," to use Mary Louise Pratt's words;[3] it is also a circular system of signification in which personal experience and geo-ethnographic knowledge mediate each other to produce a split text that simultaneously writes *about* and *against* both Oriental and orientalist cultures. These systems of meaning are further complicated by the problematics of gender in which this text as a joint production is inscribed. Throughout the text, the relations between husband and wife, traveler and writer, and ethnographer and adventurer multiply the book's subject and ideological positions, obscuring the boundaries of ethnography, travelogue, and (auto)biography. My aim in this chapter, therefore, is not to make distinctions between various modes of knowledge in this text, but to show the ways they work together to produce a discursive practice that can negotiate different, and at times contradictory, interests—interests that can range from a personal one like buying strong Arabian horses to correcting the errors in maps of Arabia for the Royal Geographical Society; or from honoring a personal promise to a Bedouin blood brother to advising British colonial officers about building railroad tracks in the Euphrates Valley.

Orientalist Authority and the Politics of Gender

Lady Anne Blunt's *Pilgrimage to Nejd* does not begin with her narrative of the voyage or her own introduction to that text but with an authoritative preface by her husband, the text's "editor" and the author of its appendixes on the history and geography of northern Arabia (figure 7). The interpolation of this "masculine" voice at the beginning points, not surprisingly, to the inequality in the relationship of this orientalist couple, a relationship in which the man occupied a position of discursive authority that sanctioned the "female" voice of the travelogue. In the gendered field of orientalist power relations where women were either excluded or made to become men's traveling appendages, a woman's representation of the exotic Other had to be authorized by a male orientalist. The relations of this orientalist couple and their coproduction were also shaped, as Billie Melman has argued,[4] by the domestic politics of nineteenth-century Britain that underlies the narrative's own rhetoric of domesticity. According to Melman, the Blunts' relationship throughout their journey in Nejd, though more liberated in many ways than those of other couples, rested on a patriarchal system of gender and familial norms that produced Wilfrid's authority over his wife. Contrary to their public image as a "pair," the Blunts' travels, she suggests, "appear to reproduce a marriage which struck even their contemporaries as an unequal partnership, a hierarchical relation, based on male domination and female deference" (283). I want to take Melman's argument a step further and suggest that Orientalism's unequal power relations not just paralleled nineteenth-century gender norms but also reaffirmed and extended these in ways that made Lady Anne doubly dependent on Wilfrid's authority. Blunt's narrative offers countless examples of how everyday practices on orientalists' journeys produced and reaffirmed a gendered division of labor. From the preparatory stage of the voyage in Damascus, where Wilfrid left Anne with cooks and the camel driver to visit bazaars, until the very last moment when his "thirst for exploration" forced the continuation of their arduous journey through Persia against his wife's wishes, the everyday life of their "campaign" was marked by a split along gendered lines between adventure and domesticity, between scientific discovery and personal experience, and between outside and inside. The journal entries for December 21, 1878, and January 11, 1879, recounting two afternoon experiences provide suggestive examples:

> Wilfrid went out for an hour this afternoon, and got some grouse, of which there are immense flocks all about the fields, while I made a picture of the town [i.e., Melakh] from behind a wall.[5]
> While I sat sketching this curious view [of a district in Jôf just before the great Nefud Desert], Wilfrid, who had climbed to the top of a tall stone, crowning the hill, came back with the news that he had discovered an inscription . . . belonging to the Greek alphabet. (1:147)

Sketch Map
of the
JEBEL SHAMMAR
by W.S.Blunt Esq.
1879

Wilfrid's symbolic ascension to the summit and his hunting while Anne sketched the panoramic view constitute typical moments in the everyday life of the orientalist couple. The male orientalist is constantly mobile and in search of adventures; the female orientalist is stationary, presumably constrained by patriarchal norms to visually record her surroundings from the domestic sphere. The ideology of adventure produces in the male orientalist an unyielding desire for exploration and discovery pursued almost always individually. The project of exotic adventure, as Victor Segalen has remarked,[6] can only be singular and individualistic—and I would add masculine. But the desire for the exotic depends for its realization on the differential role of the female companion as the stable observer and admirer of such adventures. Wilfrid's constant demand that Anne keep an eye out from a distance while he pursued his explorations suggests the significance of the woman's differential position for the realization of the male orientalist's desire for the exotic. Indeed, the narrative sections of *Pilgrimage* can be read as a showcase of Wilfrid the hunter and intrepid explorer of unknown regions with Anne in the position of the observer, the sketcher, and the recorder. The male orientalist here needs two others: the Bedouin as the object of his desire and his wife as the mediator of its fulfillment. Wilfrid's identity as a heroic adventurer can be constructed differentially only through the mediated role of Anne as the deheroicized female witness.

While the colonialist ideology of adventure splits the couple in the field into hero and scribe-witness, its relations of discursive production create a different, though still unequal, relationship between male and female orientalists in the writing scene. *Pilgrimage* belongs to a phallocentric tradition of representation in which the division of discursive labor is unabashedly demarcated along gendered lines; that is, between the woman as the fieldworker and the man as the analytical theorist. The very structure of the text makes this division symptomatically evident: the travelogue begins and ends with Wilfrid's general theories and scientific observations of Nejd, whereas Anne's travelogue, functioning as a kind of *aide-mémoire* for the theorist, is a personal narrative of their experiences in the field. Excluded from orientalist institutions such as the Royal Geographical Society—she had to sit silently beside her husband as he read

Figure 7. Map of the Jebel Shammar, by Wilfred Blunt. Reproduced from *The Proceedings of the Royal Geographical Society and Monthly Record of Geography*, vol. 2 (February 1880).

his report of their findings to the members of the Society in December 1879, as I will discuss later—Anne Blunt was compelled to occupy the subordinate and crucial, though devalorized, position of note taker and sketcher for her husband, who used her text and images to create theories and give advice to his male colleagues. There is no record of Wilfrid Blunt's own travel notes, if any, and according to one of Anne's letters to Ralph Wentworth, Wilfrid had already begun reading her notes in the spring of 1879 in Simla before their return to England.[7] The ethnographic practice of participation-observation here is split according to gender differences, between the wife who grasps the particular events of the journey and takes notes and the husband who steps back to make sense of them in his theoretical reflections. The relationship between the couple is thus made to appear as a dialectic of experience and interpretation in which Anne's experiential narrative provides the raw material for Wilfrid's authority to theorize about Bedouin culture. Wilfred's authority, in turn, sanctions the presentation and publication of Anne's travelogue.

But how does the male orientalist transform the experiential narrative of the female fieldworker into a discourse of authority that can acutely sanction the publication of her notes in the form of a travelogue? From what and where is his authority derived? What mediates the dialectic of experience and interpretation or the construction of their relationship as such? Wilfrid's orientalist authority, I want to argue, was not merely the result of an a priori patriarchal power structure reproduced in the field; it was also the effect of strategies of orientalist representation. To speak as an authoritative subject here depends not only on the experience of traveling and observation in the field as documented by the travelogue, but also on the paradigmatic and theoretical frameworks granted to the male traveler by Orientalism as an institution of power that mediates the transformation of experience into theory and narrative into description. Blunt's introductory remarks in the preface create a privileged site for the strategies of discursive empowerment which produce the effect of male orientalist authority.

To begin with, Wilfrid situates their journey to Nejd as a "natural complement" to their earlier voyage through Mesopotamia and the Syrian Desert, creating a sense of (af)filiation with a reading public that can appreciate the region's significance as an "object" of study. Blunt's remarks at once validate the "persona" of the speaker as a professional traveler and orientalist, and in so doing acknowledge the necessary rapport with his interlocutor. Although a professional orientalist, Blunt underscores his passion and "romantic interest" in the journey; he is a traveler, unlike the dispassionate administrator, "imbuded . . . with the fancies of the Desert" (1:x). To underscore his participatory role and to enhance the readers' interest in the journey, Blunt goes on to remind them of a promise he had given during an earlier journey, to his Bedouin blood brother, Mohammed Abdallah, to find him a bride from Nejd, a promise that has become a fraternal duty to be pursued in "strict accordance with Bedouin notions" (1:xi). While the rather lengthy summary of the circumstances surrounding this situation identifies Blunt as a sympathetic orientalist genuinely interested in the Other's culture, it also reaffirms his *participatory* mode of observation, which differentiates the Blunts' journey from the conventionally distant mode of travel abroad. Later, in Anne's narrative, the reader is given a full account of their participation in marital negotiations with the family of Jazi Arûk that result in a marriage contract between Mohammed and Jazi's third daughter, Muttra, whose dowry Wilfrid, the "patriarch," pays. The orientalist authority in *Pilgrimage* depends less on the separation of the investigator and the object of investigation than on the traveler's participatory observation. Blunt concludes his account of the personal circumstances of their journey by pointing out that their "singular advantage of being accepted as members of an Arabian family . . . gave us an unique occasion of seeing, and of understanding what we saw" (1:xvii). Living among the Bedouin tribes for an extended period, using their language, and experiencing their everyday cultural relations are precisely what impart authority to his discourse. Wilfrid Blunt seems, in fact, quite conscious of how claims to experience produce authority. In one of the book's most important appendixes, on the practicality of the Euphrates Valley railway, Wilfrid uses his experience as traveler to authorize his voice:

Having now completed the whole journey by land between Alexandretta and Bushire, the extreme points usually mentioned as terminuses for a Perso-Mediterranean Railway, and being, in so far, capable of estimating the real resources of the countries such a railway would serve, I make no apology for the few remarks I here offer on the subject. I do so with the more confidence because I perceive that of the many advocates these railway schemes have had, not one has taken the trouble of thus travelling over the whole distance, and that nearly all calculations made regarding them, are based on a survey of a part only of the road. (2:271)

The logic of Blunt's introductory statement is quite simple: "I can speak about the subject with authority because I have been there." Experience, in orientalist text, equals discursive authority.

Such an experiential authority depends on "the power of observation," to use James Clifford's words.[8] An authoritative traveler has the ability, or rather the "right," to see things in a way that will allow him (or her) to later step back and theorize about them. In his summary of "the profit of [their] expedition," Blunt boasts that "we are the only ones [travelers to Jebel Shammar] who have done so openly [that is, not disguised as "Orientals"] and at our leisure, provided with compass and barometer and free to take note of all we saw" (1:xvii). This is followed by a criticism of their more "serious" precursor, Gifford Palgrave, who, according to the Blunts, was "too little in sympathy with the desert to take accurate note of its details, and the circumstances of his journey [that is, traveling in the summer and mostly at night] precluded him from observing it geographically" (1:xix). This critical comparison highlights Blunt's emphasis on the visual as the most crucial aspect of their discursive practice. The Blunts' discourse belongs to an empirical mode of knowledge that privileges visual and spatial conceptualizations of the Other's culture.[9] I call the Blunts' discourse a geo-ethnography because so much of what it has to say about Bedouin culture depends on its descriptions of the geographical and spatial nature of the desert, descriptions that à la limite explain the complexity of cultural relations in Arabia. After all, let us be reminded that, as the proceedings of the Royal Geographical Society demonstrate, nineteenth-century geography as a discipline included ethnology, ethnography, and anthropology. As in the case of the traditional anthropologist, understanding the Bedouin culture here means visualizing it through such instruments as maps, charts, and tables of geographical data. Throughout their journey, not only were the Blunts concerned with the visual and aesthetic aspects of the Bedouin culture represented in Lady Anne's "conscientious representations of the chief physical features of Central Arabia" (1:xx), they were also driven by an insatiable desire to advance geographical knowledge about the Arabian Desert and correct errors in maps and descriptions of Nejd's landscape in previous accounts. Equipped with new tools for observation, the orientalist is able to visualize and produce a "graphic-spatial" account of the Other's culture. As Wilfrid himself admits, it is precisely their visual and geographic observations—exclusively produced by Anne—that "lend" an interest and authority to their narrative beyond their "personal adventures" (1:xvi).

Finally, Wilfrid's orientalist authority is derived from what Michel Foucault calls *emplacement*, or the institutional site from which the speaking subject delivers his discourse. In this case, the Royal Geographical Society was the privileged site that provided the source, the point of application, and the instruments of verification for the orientalist savant. In spite of his anticolonial stance, Wilfrid was quite blunt about his affiliation and the "profit of [their] expedition" for such institutions of knowledge and power. In his preface and in his lecture of December 8, 1879, to the Royal Geographical Society, he lists all the contributions to Orientalism of their journey through Nejd. "By taking continuous note of the variations of the barometer while [they] traveled," the Blunts were able to prove that "the plateau of Haïl is nearly twice the height supposed for it"; and by taking the "great pilgrim-road from the Euphrates," they corrected previous maps of the region (1:xx). Moreover, the Blunts did "correct a few mistakes, and . . . clear[ed] up a doubt, . . . as to the rock formation of Jebel Aja," provided "original" information about the great sand desert, and, finally, offered a very important "description of the political system of . . . Shepherd rule . . . in Central Arabia" (1:xx, xxi). Beyond their scientific value, these observations are also presented as arguments against the construction of the "Euphrates Valley" and "Indo-Mediterranean" railways by the British colonizers.

Blunt's summary and his detailed accounts of these points of application in the appendixes of the travelogue point to the significance of institutional sites as producers of empowering affiliations for nineteenth-century travelers—affiliations that in turn made these travelers valuable information collectors in the service of the institutions of power and knowledge. In other words, there was a circular system of exchange between the traveler and the *emplacement*. The institution, on the one hand, equipped the traveler with instruments of verification, such as maps and technical knowledge, enabling him or her to make systematic observations and determine more accurately the specific objects of expedition. Therefore, as a member of the Royal Geographical Society, a traveler like Blunt was able to make his general introductory statements with authority, an authority that could itself authorize the narrative that follows. In exchange, the travelers gathered new information to produce new instruments of verification to be relayed through the institution to future travelers and, ironically, for the colonialist entrepreneurial interventions that the Blunts opposed.

In summary, orientalist authority in *Pilgrimage* is the effect of a complex system of exchange between a patriarchal structure of professional relationships and certain strategies of representation granted to the travelers by Orientalism. Authority here depends simultaneously on the actual experience of traveling and observation in the field, produced through a gendered division of labor, and on the paradigmatic and theoretical frameworks that the institution of knowledge provides. The relation between these discursive poles is circular in that each mediates the other to authorize and be authorized. Lady Anne's personal narrative mediated through Orientalism's discursive strategies guarantees the authority and authenticity of Wilfrid's impersonal theories—theories that in turn authorize the production of the narrative that sanctions them.

Discourse of Discovery, Allegory of Survival

In his seminal essay, "On Ethnographic Allegory,"[10] James Clifford argues that the ethnographer's move from his oral/discursive experience in the field to a written version of such an encounter enacts the allegorical structure of "salvage." "Ethnographic pastoral," as he calls the transformation, involves an operation of representational rescue that legitimizes its practice through a claim to save the Other and his or her culture in the text and in an ethnographic present that is both romantic and redemptive. In this nostalgic story of loss and rescue, the Other is conveniently located in a "present-becoming-past," a contradictory moment that unveils the rhetorical construct producing the myth of the disappearing Other as the object of the ethnographer's representational practice. The allegorical structure of salvage underlies much of nineteenth-century Orientalism, most evidently in the works of writers like Flaubert and Nerval, who, as I argue in previous chapters, attempted to rescue the disappearing Oriental in their melancholy reflections of the journey. But in Anne Blunt's *Pilgrimage*, "ethnographic pastoral" is transformed into a discourse of discovery whose allegorical structure depends on the *survival* of the Other instead of his or her disappearance. Blunt's geo-ethnography is allegorical in that the story it tells about her particular journey through Bedouin culture implies other stories and meanings that "transcend" the original story; but her representational practice depends less on a position of otherness as a "present-becoming-past" than on the possibility of past-becoming-present for the traveler. *Pilgrimage*, therefore, is not so much a nostalgic allegory of loss and rescue as it is a hopeful, though romantic, discourse of discovery that finds among Bedouins qualities the Blunts consider lost from European culture—qualities such as the affinity for the pastoral and nature, genuine hospitality, social forbearance, religious piety, and so on. This allegory of survival, if I may call it that, is ideologically ambivalent because it enacts both the orientalist tendency to search for origin and authenticity in the Orient—for example, in the romantic idea that Europe's disappearing past is still present in the "primitive" Other—and the "unorientalist" desire to embrace the Other and his or her culture without falling into the trap of nativism. As in the allegory of ethnographic rescue, Blunt's representation of Bedouin culture as pastoral implies an unconscious sense of orientalist nostalgia, and yet her valorization of Bedouins also involves a critical attitude toward Europe's claims to rescue as she seeks local knowledge and learns about their everyday life. In this section, I explore how these opposing poles of representation inform each other, thus allowing the emergence of an ethnographic description that is understanding of cultural difference and yet still embedded in colonialist relations of power.

As a piece of Victorian exploration writing, *Pilgrimage* falls back on the familiar discourse of discovery to accomplish its representational task. From the very beginning of the journey, when she forewarns the reader that "Nejd, in the imagination of the Northern Arabs, is an immense way off, and no one has ever been known to go there from Damascus" (1:5), until the very end, where she boasts as a heroic adventurer that "we [have] now done what few if any Europeans [have] done before" (2:229), her narrative is contrived, indeed regulated, by the rhetoric of discovery that underscores the uniqueness of the traveler's endeavor, making her ethnographic descriptions function as records of discovery. Inscribed in the tradition of heroic adventure, the discourse of discovery construes the journey as a challenge that the adventurous traveler must overcome. As in other Victorian travelogues, geographical, psychological, logistic, and political obstacles occupy a privileged position in Blunt's narrative. In the very beginning of her travelogue, for example, Anne distinguishes their journey from a "pleasure trip" and describes it as an extremely "serious" effort launched with "considerable risk" to explore a barren region "where it was impossible to count upon fresh supplies even of the commonest necessaries of life" (1:21). She then goes on to explain how they prepare for a "campaign" for which they "could not afford to leave anything to chance" (ibid.). Throughout the narrative, the reader is often made aware of the travelers' trials. Anne recounts in great detail the difficulties of moving through the deep sand of the Nefud Desert, their suffering from hunger and thirst, and their being attacked by guides turned robbers.

The theme of hardship is crucial to the discourse of discovery because it fulfills the ideological function of valorizing the orientalist as the heroic adventurer, and therefore brings Anne Blunt back into a tradition from which she is written out in the everyday life of the orientalist journey. Here, she, like the male orientalists, is an intrepid adventurer who embarks on a difficult journey, overcomes the "hostile" world, and triumphantly brings back home strategic information or knowledge about the Other. Obstacles of the voyage and the traveler's mastery over them conjure the sense of heroism that Orientalism's ideology of adventure promises. In fact, there is a desperate need to have adventures in the journey: "Friday, January 3.—We have had an adventure *at last*" (1:102; my emphasis). Pain as opposed to pleasure, work in contrast to leisure, and hardship as against comfort are precisely what distinguish the orientalist adventurer from the tourist; these are the marks of "serious" adventure that foreground the voyage of discovery within a heroic perspective. In short, the theme of hardship provides the very conditions of meaningfulness for Blunt's voyage to Nejd, evoking a Western heroic tradition whose allegorical function differentiates their travel from a leisure trip.

The thematics of trial and hardship are also crucial to the *Pilgrimage's* mode of textualization in that, as a framing device for geo-ethnographic descriptions, they valorize the otherwise unheroic act of observation. The act of discovery in Victorian exploration writing, as Mary Louise Pratt has suggested,[11] consists, ironically, of the passive experience of seeing; but the traveler renders this "nonevent" significant by dramatizing his or her passage to the unknown region. Pratt goes on to argue that "while the ordeal required to make the discovery is unforgettably concrete, in the mid-Victorian Paradigm the 'discovery' itself, even within the ideology of discovery, has no existence of its own. It only gets 'made' for real after the traveler (or other survivor) returns home, and brings it into being through texts: a name on a map, a report to the Royal Geographical Society, the Foreign Office, the London Mission Society, a diary, a lecture, a travel book" (204).

"Discovery," in other words, is a discursive phenomenon that glamorizes the traveler's observation into heroic action. The dramatic moment of the Blunts' "discovery" of Jebel Shammar illustrates the transformation of the visual into action:

January 23.—It is like a dream to be sitting here, writing a journal on a rock in Jebel Shammar. When I remember how, years ago, I read that romantic account by Mr. Palgrave, which nobody believed, of an ideal State in the heart of Arabia, and a happy land which nobody but he had seen, and how impossibly remote and unreal it all appeared; and how, later during our travels, we heard of Nejd and Haïl and this very Jebel Shammar, spoken of with a kind of awe by all who knew the name, even by the Bedouins, from the day when at Aleppo Mr. S. firstanswered our vague questions about it by saying, "It is possible to go there. Why do you not go?" I feel that we have achieved something which it is not given to every one to do. Wilfrid declares that he shall die happy now, even if we have our heads cut off at Haïl. It is with him a favorite maxim, that every place is exactly like every other place, but Jebel Shammar is not like anything else, at least that I have seen in this world, unless it be Mount Sinaï, and it is more beautiful than that. (1:207–8)

The euphoria, almost ecstasy, expressed by Lady Anne on seeing Jebel Shammar is prefaced by her note on how impossibly remote, and hence unreal, the site had been in the traveler's imagination, making the mere act of seeing seem like a dramatic achievement. She underscores the uniqueness and special beauty of Jebel Shammar and draws attention to her sense of victory at having accomplished what only a few have done before. There is indeed a sense of conquest and triumph in her euphoric reflections that renders the otherwise passive experience of viewing the scenery a heroic deed. This journal entry also provides a fascinating example of how the ideology of adventure was disseminated in Victorian culture. As in the case of Nerval, Anne's desire to see and write about Jebel Shammar was mediated by an orientalist intertext that made the journey through one of the most difficult and remote regions of the world a fantasy. The Blunts' euphoria demonstrates the decisive role of orientalist discourse in the production of the ideology of adventure in Victorian culture. Although Anne uses the earlier moment of reading and dreaming to highlight her actual ascent to Jebel Shammar, the act of reading has functioned as a powerful force engendering the desire to master the impossible—not to mention, of course, that the act of writing has inscribed her into orientalist history and into the body of intertexts' for other readers.

The mediating function of the orientalist intertext, however, is not ideologically monolithic: writing *through* the intertext always involves a gesture of writing *against* it. The new representation always defines its discursive project differentially and therefore includes in its repertoire counterterms. *Pilgrimage's* revision of Palgrave's account often embodies a corrective mode that demystifies his vision of Arabia. Blunt's description of Nefud is a case in point:

> January 13.—We have been all day in the Nefûd, which is interesting beyond our hopes, and charming into the bargain. It is moreover, quite unlike the description I remember to have read of it by Mr. Palgrave, which affects one as a nightmare of impossible horror. It is true he passed it in summer, and we are now in mid-winter, but the physical features cannot be much changed by the change of seasons, and I cannot understand how he overlooked its main characteristics. . . . It is tufted all over with ghada bushes, and bushes of another kind called *yerta*, which at this time of the year when there are no leaves, is exactly like a thickly matted vine. . . . The rasúl Allah (God's prophet), Radi says, came one day to a place where there was a vineyard, and found some peasants pruning. He asked them what they were doing, and what the trees were, and they, fearing his displeasure or to make fun of him, answered, these are "yerta" trees, yerta being the first name that came into their heads. "Yerta inshallah, yerta let them be then," rejoined the prophet, and from that day forth they ceased to be vines and bore no fruit. . . . Instead of being the terrible place it has been described by the few travellers who have seen it, it is in reality the home of the Bedouins during a great part of the year. Its only want is water, for it contains but few wells; all along the edge, it is thickly inhabited, and Radi tells us that in the spring, when the grass is green after rain, the Bedouins care nothing for water, as their camels are in milk, and they go for weeks without it, wandering far into the interior of the sand desert. (1:156, 158)

The revisionary passage is on the surface a correction of Palgrave's representation of Nefud as Lady Blunt corrects his observational errors; as such, it is consistent with the colonialist practice of information collecting. But this journal entry also implies a subtle critique of Palgrave's ethnocentric and negative views of Arabia, depicting Nefud not as a "nightmare of impossible horror" but as the "charming" home of Bedouin tribes whose adaptation to the physical features of the desert allows them to inhabit comfortably the seemingly barren region. Her description, unlike Palgrave's, is free of metaphor and adjectival modifiers and does not posit a relation of mastery between the European onlooker and the object, as do the accounts by male Victorian travelers. Anne's narrative also seems acutely aware that Bedouins view the region differently, and she includes their perspective in her representation. She incorporates, for example, Radi's mythological story about the origin of *yerta* and the way Bedouins manage the shortage of water without either questioning their validity or imposing an authoritative voice. One encounters here a desire to understand the local knowledge, neither attempting to rationalize, as her husband Wilfrid often does, everything according to Western theories and assumptions, nor to claim the power of possessing it, as most Victorian travelers did.

Anne's interest in local knowledge is also apparent in her descriptions of everyday life in Bedouin tribes. Even though her discursive practice is clearly embedded in the network of colonial relations, her representations of Arabian culture, unlike those of Charles Doughty and Palgrave, work out of a dialogic consciousness that seeks out local knowledge, to use Pratt's words. This is most evident in the account of her visit to Ibn Rashid's harem in Haïl. I have argued elsewhere that the harem, as a prevalent literary topos in orientalist literature, has been central to the eroticization of the Orient, representing and fulfilling Europe's fantasies of boundless sexuality and desire for domination.[12] But Blunt's representation of the harem is anything but erotic and violent. On the second day after her arrival in Haïl, she asked the emir if she might visit his harem, a request that was immediately granted. Later, a servant informed her that Amusheh, the emir's chief wife, was ready to receive her and led Anne to the women's quarter. Significantly, her narrative neither dramatizes the harem's inaccessibility nor valorizes her visit as a symbolic "penetration" into a sacred and secretive domain, as do previous accounts by men. Anne characterizes the visit as a mundane social event where the guest, as anywhere else, is entertained by the host. There is even a tendency in her narrative to deeroticize. Consider, for example, her description of the women's dresses and jewelry, a familiar trope in Western representation of the harem:

> Each lady had a garment cut like an abba, but closed up the front, so that it must have been put on over the head; and as it was worn without any belt or fastening at the waist, it had the effect of a sack. These

sacks or bags were of magnificent material, gold interwoven with silk, but neither convenient nor becoming, effectually hiding any grace of figure. . . . [The nose ring] consists of a thin circle of gold, with a knot of gold and turquoises attached by a chain to the cap or lappet before described. It is worn in the left nostril, but taken out and left dangling while the wearer eats and drinks. A most inconvenient ornament, I thought and said, and when removed it leaves an unsightly hole, badly pierced, in the nostril, and more uncomfortable-looking than the holes in European ears. But fashion rules the ladies at Haïl as in other places, and my new acquaintances only laughed at such criticisms. They find these trinkets useful toys, and amuse themselves while talking by continually pulling them out and putting them in again. The larger size of ring seemed besides to be a mark of high position, so that the diameter of the circle might be considered the measure of the owner's rank. (1:234–36)

One is struck immediately in reading this passage by Anne's lack of interest in using descriptions of women's clothing and jewelry as a vehicle to stimulate male erotic desires. Far from providing the saturated effect of ornamentation that renders the women of the harem dreamy and desirable objects of voyeurism in orientalist erotic literature, the above description actually creates an unerotic effect. One can still detect here the orientalist's positivist tendency to take pleasure in scrutinizing and enumerating the women's articles of clothing and ornamentations, but Anne's images undermine the male reader's scopic desires, especially the desire to indulge in metonymies of orientalist erotica, by pointing out, from a Western perspective, the inconvenience and unattractiveness of wearing an abba and nose ring. Although Anne expresses her personal opinions about women's dresses and jewelry, she remains nonetheless sensible to differences in fashion and the fact that standards of beauty are culturally constructed. Her recording of the women's laughter at her criticism and the relation between the size of the nose ring and prestige underscore her recognition of cultural differences.

Anne's comment about the ubiquity of fashion, cliché though it may seem, establishes also a moment of ambivalence in which the ethnographic present is problematized. Exploration writing, as a colonialist discourse, has a tendency to place the Other in a time other than the present of the traveler-speaker, as Fabian has demonstrated. But Anne's comment implies an "intersubjective time" that destabilizes the mode of distancing the traveler from the Other so prevalent in Victorian travel writing. This and other similar statements, not to mention Anne's genuine interest in comprehending local knowledge, suggest an understanding of communication and representation as sharing time, as a temporal and social relation between the observer and the observed.

Crucial to the destabilization of the ethnographic present is the traveler's emphasis on contextualizing the very act of writing. Anne often records moments of sitting in a corner or on a promontory and writing in her pocket diary about what she has seen—notes such as, "I profit by the quiet thus secured, and by the last hour of daylight to write my journal" (2:178); or, "with the first light, we went on through the town and stopped again in front of the Seraï. Here I have been writing my journal and sketching the picturesque old palace" (2:222). No doubt these notes are meant to give her narrative a sense of immediacy, and they attest to her orientalist desire to "capture" the reality of the moment in a discourse driven by a will to truth. But they can also be read as self-reflexive moments that underscore the intersubjective and contextual nature of ethnographic practice. The recording of these moments inscribes the I/eye in her representation. For, unlike other exploration writings that deny the social and temporal contexts of representation through claims of objectivity, distancing the speaker from the "referent," Lady Anne Blunt's text brings to focus her subjectivity and the condition of her writing. Self-reflexive moments in *Pilgrimage* are textual memories that make the reader remember what is often denied in exploration writing: the shared time (coevalness) of the traveler and the Other, and the (inter)subjectivity of representation.

Male Orientalism, Female Orientalist

Among the fellows of the Royal Geographical Society who responded to Wilfrid Blunt's report on the voyage to Nejd (December 8, 1879) was Sir Henry Rawlinson, a prominent orientalist and member of the Foreign Office. His congratulatory remarks provide an interesting context in which to consider the relation of Lady Anne Blunt's travelogue to the general system of orientalist discursive productions.

Arabia was a country in which [Rawlinson] had always taken great interest; and all Eastern travellers must have shared the same feeling. There was a sort of weird mystery about it, from the difficulty of penetrating into it and the character of its inhabitants. Jebel Shammar, especially during the twelve years he was at Bagdad, always exercised a particular influence on his imagination. There was at that time great difficulty in reaching the country. The medical man attached to the Residency in those days, Mr. John Ross, a great traveller and a perfect Arabic scholar, had been over the whole of the Mesopotamian Desert, and he had penetrated into many of the nooks and corners of Arabia; but he was never able to reach the Jebel Shammar.... He congratulated [Wilfrid] sincerely on his journey, and if Lady Anne would permit him he would congratulate her also. It is a most surprising thing for an English lady to mount horse at Palmyra and Damascus and ride through Arabia, passing through a district which the experienced doctor he had mentioned never could reach, and then turning back by the Caliph route. It was a most astonishing exploit, not merely satisfactory to herself but to the nation which possessed a lady of such a character.[13]

Rawlinson's laudatory remarks are interesting in themselves as an expression of the male's epistemophilic desire to "penetrate into" the unknown and expose it. The orientalist reaffirms the myth of primitivism and the colonialist will to knowledge and power. Arabia, in Rawlinson's crudely orientalist view, is an enigmatically mysterious region whose inaccessibility only fuels his desire to know and "unveil." Rawlinson's statements also bring into focus the blatantly patriarchal structure of orientalist institutions of knowledge. Although it was Lady Anne who gathered the information about Nejd in the ten volumes of her journals and pocket diary, and produced the drawings of the trip—which were, incidentally, displayed on a table during Wilfrid's presentation as a "treat" for the fellows of the Royal Geographical Society—she occupied a secondary position to the male orientalist, having had to sit silently next to her husband, who unabashedly presented their findings as his own scientific discoveries. Anne was recognized merely for traveling in Arabia as a woman, while Wilfrid was acknowledged as the scientist and discoverer. In the patriarchal system of Orientalism, the female traveler is the excluded Other who is included only as the token exception in a field defined as masculine.

In the context of such an epistemophilic and patriarchal field of knowledge, as expressed so well in Rawlinson's remarks, the implications of Anne Blunt's discursive ambivalence become more readable. *Pilgrimage's* representation of Arabia is at least twice inscribed, for it has to work both within the conventions of orientalist discourses and against their mono-logic and authoritative tendencies. Even a marginalized female traveler like Anne Blunt could not avoid the cultural authority and epistemologi-cal baggage of Orientalism. Her desire for knowledge about Arabia, her participation in the ideology of adventure, and the discourse of discovery in her narrative demonstrate the impossibility of occupying a position outside the orientalist formation. For not only did institutions such as the Royal Geographical Society and the Foreign Office provide travelers like the Blunts with technical knowledge and instruments to explore "unknown" regions such as central Arabia, but Orientalism as a cultural force—as Rawlinson's case demonstrates—produced the "romantic inter-est" that induced Victorian travelers to embark on such adventures. Travel writing, whether produced by men or by women, therefore is always an (af)filiated discourse: it maintains both an institutional affiliation with colonial power and a kind of "filial" relation with other orientalist repre-sentations.

But orientalist (af)filiation, while it is inescapable and restrictive, is also productive of change and divergence. This is especially true in the case of travelers like Anne Blunt, whose marginal location as a woman in the field of Orientalism seems to have engendered a dialogic consciousness that marks in her representational practice an elusive shift away from some of the dominant strains of scientific Orientalism. Self-reflexivity in writing about culture, interest in local knowledge, and sensitivity to coevalness with Bedouins are instances of discontinuity from dominant orientalist discourses. These shifts suggest that the constitution and production of orientalist knowledge is informed by the enabling effects of difference and divergence. Anne Blunt's narrative does not question the legitimacy of dominant orientalist modes of representation, but it employs them in ways that deflect their authority and mediate new possibilities for repre-sentation. Reinscription of orientalist authority, in other words, is always productive of change.

But these discursive shifts, it must be emphasized, are produced within the orientalist system as part of its discursive apparatus, and as such, ironically, they do not necessarily destabilize the prevailing practice of authority but strengthen it. To the extent that discursive shifts have a transformative function, they are needed by Orientalism as formative ele-ments through whose mediation the system restructures and refashions itself. *Pilgrimage*, for example, is not antithetical to male orientalist discourses of discovery and adventure, as I have shown; rather, it constitutes a *differential* text in relation to them, a text that posits a difference but whose effects are reappropriated within the larger system of orientalist discursive production. Anne Blunt's discursive practice and her enthusiastic reception by the Royal Geographical Society demonstrate that difference is the sign of productivity in the colonialist system of knowledge and power, that strategies of domination are often produced differentially, and that the divisive desire for the Other can always be reimplicated in the ideology of adventure and the discourses of discovery.

6. *Allahou Akbar! He Is a Woman*: Colonialism, Transvestism, and the Orientalist Parasite

✸

The parasite is the site and subject of transformation.—Michel Serres, Le parasite

In an intellectual climate in which the death of the author has become a theoretical truism, to read and write biographically as I intend to do in this chapter seems a naive, if not a "backward," exercise. And yet, faced with an ostensibly autobiographical text such as Isabelle Eberhardt's, I cannot resist the temptation to imagine the persona behind it and to try to understand her historical significance in this context. Eberhardt's writing withstands critical distance; its iconic aura invites a(n) (auto)biographical interest that induces one to read the text in relation to its subject's image repertoire.[1] As I read her journals, notes, and stories, I cannot separate myself from the *imaginary* of Eberhardt's life that intrigues me and makes me "interested" in *her*—a kind of *auto*biographical identification, for example, with her scandalous adventures, her self-fashioning through exile, and her dislocation and melancholic vagabondage. As a "personification of displacement,"[2] Isabelle's "imaginary" displaces for a moment my critical interest, inducing instead a personal desire, in my own writing, to experience a crossing of racial and gender boundaries. The biographical interest in Eberhardt's work is thus a kind of *auto*biographical interest displaced as a practice of writing about an Other's life, an Other's journey. For me, telling the story of someone else's voyage to the Orient involves a trajectory of identifying a complex set of subjective relations that challenge such binary distinctions as self/other, man/woman, Orient/Occident, colonizer/colonized.

To write (auto)biographically, however, does not suggest a narcissistic mode of reading in which the Other becomes an alibi for a vulgar self-identification—the autobiographical references can only be acknowledged, never spelled out. Nor does my reading imply a valorization of the author, as a privileged originating subject, at the cost of the text itself. For Eberhardt does not occupy a privileged moment in her texts' modes of being.[3] What is at stake here is a kind of contextualization that bridges the theoretical gap created by the depoliticized reception of poststructuralism in the North American academy between discourse as practice and the enunciative subject as practitioner.[4] My recourse to biographic and historical details is not meant to undermine the text itself but to emphasize its status as a specific social practice, a system of dependencies in which the speaking subject is a variable.[5] Embedded in the historical reality of the French Empire, the account of Eberhardt's political and personal involvement in North Africa unavoidably demands a contextualized treatment that crosses the boundaries of textuality, subjectivity, gender, and historicity.[6]

In what follows, therefore, I will consider a period of seven years, 1897–1904, during which Eberhardt spent most of her time in North Africa, living—mostly in the guise of an Oriental man—an adventurous life of vagabondage, mysticism, and, eventually, colonial participation. During this period, driven by an insatiable desire to make a literary name for herself, Eberhardt wrote numerous short stories, notes, diaries, journalistic articles, and a novel, most of which were extensively edited by Victor Barrucand and Réné-Louis Doyon and published posthumously in La Dépêche Algérienne and other colonial journals. Given my biographical orientation in this chapter, I will concentrate on Eberhardt's "nonfiction" works to construct her image repertoire as an orientalist subject adrift. What I encounter in these autobiographical texts is not so much a mode of representation of the Oriental Other as the figuration of a self adrift in the Other—it is a mode of writing that does not exoticize the Orient but articulates its difference in the subjective profile of an orientalist encounter.[7] Her discourse, in other words, is a mode of articulation that imposes a "failure of distinction," to use Marjorie Garber's words, a way of representing that constantly blurs, while simultaneously reaffirming, the representational boundaries of the orientalist and the Oriental, the colonizer and the colonized.

Inscribed within the political economy of Orientalism, Eberhardt's figurational discourse is of a "parasitic" order and is therefore politically ambivalent. My use of the term parasite here is a parasitic use of Michel Serres's notion. He uses the word in its polysemy—the biological parasite (i.e., the organism that feeds off another living organism), the social parasite (i.e., the overbearing guest), and the communicational parasite (the static or the noise in a channel of communication)—to demonstrate how the figure of the parasite disrupts a system by violating the structure of exchange, but in doing so creates a new and more complex order. As a "third category," the parasite resembles the figure of the transvestite in that it constitutes a disruptive element that intervenes in cultural exchanges by challenging their binary logic. But the parasitic transvestite, I will argue, is a split subject whose ambivalence makes him or her vulnerable to recuperation by the colonial system—General Lyautey, as I will discuss later, literally recovered Eberhardt's *Sud-Oranais* from the rubble left by the flood that drowned her in 1904. As the articulation of a scandalous identification with the Other, Eberhardt's works, on the one hand, are *noise* in the orientalist-colonialist discourse, disturbing its order and disavowing its oppressive power relations. And yet, because of their knowledge of the Other and as a testimony to the strategic limitations of colonial order, her texts are transformed into a source of information for the colonial power they oppose, allowing the system to produce a new and more efficient colonial order. In this sense, I disagree with Garber's claim about the transgressive nature of Eberhardt's colonial encounter by arguing that the orientalist transvestite is the included third party between the colonizer and the colonized whose mediating role actually ensures a smooth transformation of power relations between them.

Displacement and the Desire for the Orient

Isabelle Eberhardt was a displaced figure from birth. Born out of wedlock in 1877 in Geneva to an exiled Russian aristocrat mother, Nathalie de Moerder, and her secret lover and the tutor of her children, Alexander Trophimowsky, Isabelle was raised and educated like a boy by her unacknowledged father in the confined atmosphere of the Villa Neuve. Needless to say, this education kindled an insatiable escapist desire for an "elsewhere" in Isabelle. As an adolescent she learned about Islam, and she learned Arabic from her anarchist tutor-father.[8] Also during this period, she discovered Pierre Loti's orientalist work, in which she found a solace for her exilic confinement. Loti's melancholy reflections, his profound sense of escapism in the Other, and his exotic depictions of the Orient as a desirable counterpart to decadent fin-de-siècle Europe offered Isabelle a locus of orientalist reverie.[9] To complement her literary vision, she began to correspond with a Tunisian civil servant, Ali Abdul-Wahab, and a

French officer, Eugène Letord, who informed her, respectively, about Islam and the geopolitical situation of North Africa, thus dilating her desire to travel in the Maghreb.

Her dream of living in the Orient came true in May 1887 when she and her mother joined Augustin, her half-brother, in Algiers. They settled in the old Arab quarter of the city and converted to Islam. The move constituted a moment of *épanouissement* for Isabelle and inspired her to write a series of sketches depicting images of local life in Algiers for the magazine *L'Athénée*. This euphoric period, however, came to a quick end. Mme. de Moerder died in November 1897, which left Isabelle in a state of shock and, later, in an "abyss of sadness" that haunted her throughout her short life. After a turbulent year of romance with a Turkish diplomat in Geneva and a series of promiscuous relations in port cities,[10] she returned to North Africa after Trophimowsky's death in May 1899 liberated her from the filial role of caretaker. Dressed as a sailor, she took a boat to Tunis, then rented a small house in the Arab quarter of the city where she could indulge in her "dream of the old Orient." "Heures de Tunis," "Au pays des sables," and "Un automne dans le Sahel tunisien" provide a detailed account of her life during this period.

As a discourse of orientalist initiation, these texts are in a "parasitic" relation to the discourses of earlier orientalists such as Loti and Nerval. They recount the experience of a belated traveler's escapist fascination with a vision of the Orient as a locus of personal emancipation, a geographical alternative that can transcend the "cruel decadence" of late nineteenth-century France. Eberhardt's Orient is a desirable Other, not an alien world, a place where she can avoid not only the "evils" of Europe's "social machine" but her own psychological conflicts. As a belated traveler overwhelmed by a desire for the Orient, mediated through orientalist intertexts, Eberhardt often describes in a romantic tone the pleasures afforded her by the Maghreb with its "eternal melancholia," "sweet joys of dawns," and "pinnacles of evenings," all of which provide a "singular sensation of appeasement" in the young orientalist.[11]

Displaced as she was, Eberhardt valorized her vagabondage in the Orient as a negation of "the proper" and a disavowal of the European order. As many readers have pointed out, Eberhardt abhorred systematization and attempted to avoid the disciplinary institutions of Europe through her nomadic life and adventures in the Orient. Convinced that "wandering [le vagabondage] is emancipation; . . . it is liberty," she went to Tunis to pursue her "dream of the old Orient, radiant and gloomy, in the old white districts full of darkness and of silence" (27, 29). Dressed in the "egalitarian costume of Bedouins," she could indulge herself in "the voluptuousness of dreaming" without any sense of guilt (29, 30). Profoundly fascinated by nomadic life, Eberhardt viewed any kind of stability as a threat to her subjectivity. To have had "a home, a family, and property or a public office" would have made her "an appreciable cogwheel of the social machine," for these are nothing but a "different form of slavery which constrains us from contact with our own fellow creatures" (28).

Eberhardt's nomadism, however, is ideologically split, for it simultaneously subverts and falls within the patriarchal and colonialist logic. At least on the surface, Eberhardt's repudiation of Western culture conveys a double critique of the bourgeois valorization of the family structure ("*la bonne famille*") and the orientalist stereotypes of European superiority over Oriental backwardness. Eberhardt's sense of *dépaysement* seems to have provided her with a critical vision, allowing her to be the noise in the orientalist system which produced her as a figure of its discontent. Speaking from the "margins" of Western rationalism, Eberhardt's Orientalism carries a slothful contestation against Occidental reality and disavows its metaphysical will to order and regulation through constructions of such disciplinary institutions as home and family. To be adrift, especially as a parasitic transvestite, is in this instance a form of political protest against the European system of social control and its phallocentric will to power.

But this very idealist critique of European consciousness is ironically articulated through an unconscious use of the language of empire, a mode of articulation that reinscribes her rebellion within the systems of power she was attempting to transcend:

> Which lord can rival him in his *power* and *opulence*?
> His *Stronghold* has no limits and his *empire* no *law*.
> No *bondage* diminishes his appeal, no toil bends his spine toward *the earth which he owns and which gives itself to him, completely, in indulgence* and in beauty.
> [Quel châtelain peut rivaliser avec lui en *puissance* et en *opulence*?
> *Son fief n'a pas de limites, et son empire pas de loi.*
> Aucun *servage* n'avilit son allure, aucun labeur ne courbe son échine vers *la terre qu'il possède et qui se donne à lui, toute, en bonté et en* beauté]. (27; my emphasis)

Eberhardt's use of masculine pronouns and an "imperialist" vocabulary to describe her "free" spirit and desire for wandering point to her discur-

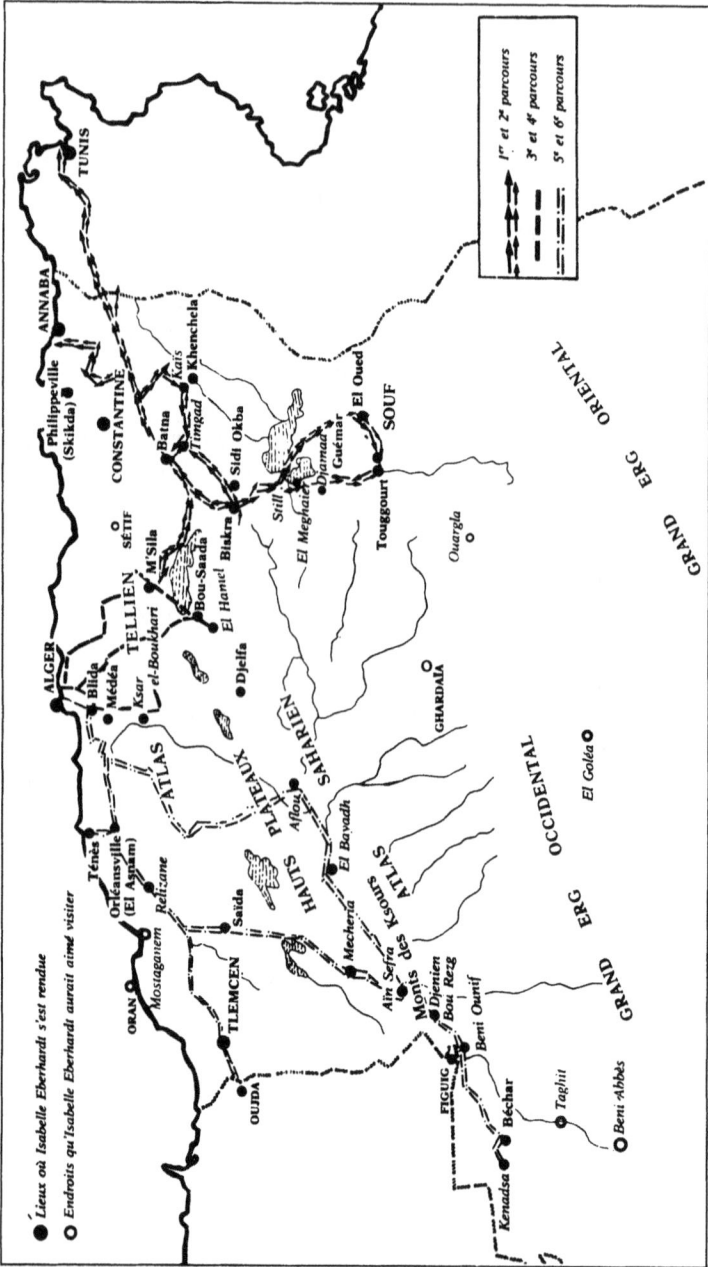

1ʳ et 2ᵉ parcours
3ᵉ et 4ᵉ parcours
5ᵉ et 6ᵉ parcours

TUNIS
ANNABA
Philippeville (Skikda)
CONSTANTINE
Kais
Khenchela
Batna
Timgad
Sidi Okba
El Oued
SOUF
Djamaa
Guémar
Biskra
Still
El Meghaïer
Touggourt
SÉTIF
M'Sila
Bou-Saada
El Hamel
Ouargla
TELLIEN
el-Boukhari
Djelfa
ALGER
Blida
Médéa
Ksar
GHARDAÏA
SAHARIEN
ATLAS
PLATEAUX
Aflou
El Bayadh
El Golea
ERG OCCIDENTAL
Ténès
Orléansville (El Asnam)
Relizane
HAUTS des KSOURS ATLAS
Saïda
Mécheria
Ain Sefra
Monts des Ksours
Mostaganem
ORAN
TLEMCEN
Djenien Bou Rezg
Beni Ounif
FIGUIG
OUJDA
Béchar
Taghit
Beni-Abbès
Kenadsa
GRAND ERG OCCIDENTAL
GRAND ERG ORIENTAL

● Lieux où Isabelle Eberhardt s'est rendue
○ Endroits qu'Isabelle Eberhardt aurait aimé visiter

sive limitations in articulating a new practice of orientalist encounter. There is no "outside" to the language of empire, and therefore the noise of contestation can be produced only within the parameters of its discursive system. To put it slightly differently, the desire to overcome the boundaries of law is mediated by the orientalist desire for knowledge and power and so unwittingly implies a return to the law's discursive regulation. The transgressive vagabond can articulate her freedom only in masculine terms and through the oppressive structure of the empire and its stronghold, her pleasure of marginality according to the power of the dominator, and her desire for freedom within the boundaries of the proper. There is no obstacle to prevent the emancipated vagabond from appropriating the infinite space in front of her. Locating herself in the position of the colonizer, she is in *control* and in possession of the "free" land.

But to say that there is no outside to the language of empire—or to its power relations—does not imply that the orientalist parasite is condemned to mere reiteration of the colonial discourse. Rather, it defines the desire for the Orient as noise arising within the discourse of Orientalism. In other words, as a mediated phenomenon, the desire for the Orient is necessarily structured according to the logic of orientalist desire for power and knowledge. Consequently, I suggest that the possibility of the articulation of this noise as a kind of counterdiscourse—taking the form of a desired *identification* with the Orient that is the *object* of orientalist knowledge—is interwoven with the relations of colonial power, which at once effect and are affected by the noise. Eberhardt's orientalist parasitism depends on the discourse and the power it tries to elude, and as a result, it is vulnerable to recuperation by that discourse and power. Let me demonstrate this point more concretely by considering Eberhardt's involvement with a group of colonial agents during her trip to the Tunisian coast (figure 8).

Traveling with the Colonizers

Besieged by one of her frequent "crises morales," Isabelle decided to take a train journey in the fall of 1899 along the southeastern coast of Tunisia,

Figure 8. Isabelle Eberhardt's travels in North Africa.
Reproduced from Eberhardt's *Ecrits sur le Sable* (Paris: Grasset, 1988), by permission of Editions Bernard Grasset.

"without knowing anyone there, purposelessly and without haste" (48).
Poor and vagrant, she tagged along with a native colonial agent, Si Elarhby,
and later a group of Spahis, whom she "parasited":[12] "For two months, I
am a witness to what these people—whom I have known only since I
have been traveling with them—do, and living their life [the nomadic
life/the parasitic life] [vivant de leur vie]" (56). This parasitic relationship
of dependency with Elarhby and the group of Spahis is an instance of
Eberhardt's political ambivalence toward the French Empire, since it extended to collaboration with the purposes of expedition. Bored with her
aimlessness, she decided to assist Elarhby in the coercive task of collecting
medjba, a head tax imposed on the native population by the French colonial system. Although conscious of her "bad deed," she acted "reluc-
tantly" as a clerk (greffier), helping the native colonial agent to imprison
poor natives and confiscate their properties for nonpayment of taxes. At
the same time, however, her participation in the oppressive act exposed
her to the harsh consequences of colonialism, raising her consciousness
to the point of reporting in an anticolonialist rhetoric the widespread
misery and discontent extending throughout the Tunisian coast—a misery to which, ironically, she herself contributed. She describes in great
detail how "women in tears bring their last goat, their last ewe," while
their men, "a glum and resigned band of chained men," are taken away
(52). Eberhardt's involvement with the colonial agents, in short, produced
an effect of opposition to French rule. In fact, in "Souvenirs du Sahel
tunisien," she appears as a firm opponent of colonialism:

> I had a chance, in the course of my peregrinations in Tunisia, to
> notice once again how hollow are in reality the striking and ele-
> gant phrases whose politics rigs itself out and justifies all of its self-
> interested, as well as egotistic, intrigues [phrases such as "the civil-
> izing and peacemaking work of France in Africa," "the beneficial
> deeds of civilization bestowed on the indigenous people of our colo-
> nies"]. . . . In Tunisia, notably, the protectorate is nothing but a euphe-
> mism concealing the total annexation, born elsewhere out of an ab-
> solute necessity." (64)

Eberhardt's resolute anticolonial statement is too explicit to need further
elaboration, but it provides an interesting example of how opposition to
colonialism is produced intrinsically at the point where power is exercised. Located between the colonial agent and the colonized, the orientalist parasite is an odd element in the field of their power relations, the

third category who creates the noise of contestation. For neither are the oppressed natives in a position to mutiny in this instance, nor are the colonizers interested in reform. The noise in the colonial system is therefore produced by the included third party: the parasite who feeds on the system and produces a discourse of discontent in exchange.

The Parasite as Transvestite

If Eberhardt was able to occupy this intermediary position in the colonial relation, it was mostly because of her split identity, inscribed not only, as an orientalist parasite, within the structure of colonial power by virtue of an economy of "Oriental" desire that contested it but also, as a transvestite, within the patriarchal structure of the gender roles that undermine the feminization of the Orient by the Occident. The orientalist parasite is located at the point where the relations of colonial power produce the effect of a desire to immerse in or be the Other—a seemingly transgressive identification that renders her identity split. Crucial to such a parasitic function is Eberhardt's ambivalent subjectivity as a transvestite, for, as I have already suggested, cross-dressing as a category crisis of male and female involves a split economy which simultaneously obeys the law and transgresses it, an ambivalence that, while mirroring her parasitic role, contributes to her mediating function within the binary logic of colonialism. Let me elaborate on this relation by considering Eberhardt's own ambivalence toward her cross-dressing (figure 9).

She seemed, on the one hand, utterly conscious of the dislocation between her female European self and the male Oriental role she adopted. This is apparent in her insistent acknowledgment of her "assumed identity" (personnalité d'emprunt) as a transvestite (51). Often she points out in her writing that "nobody knows my true identity," thus acknowledging a split between her "real" self and her adopted identity, an acknowledgment that underlines her recognition of gender as a constructed category as well as the split between her cultural and physical identities (61; my emphasis).

In "Vers les horizons bleus," she even goes so far as to rationalize her orientalist masquerade as a strategic necessity:

In the proper dress of a European young lady, I would have never seen anything; the world would have been closed to me, because the exterior life seems to have been made for the man and not for the woman. However, I like to dive into the bath of popular life, to feel

Figure 9. Allahou-Akbar! He is a woman. Reproduced by permission of François Cominardi.

the wave of the crowd flow over me, and to become impregnated with the fluids of the masses. Only in this manner I possess a city and know it in ways that the tourist will never understand, despite all the explanations of his guides.

[Sous un costume correcte de jeune fille européenne, je n'aurais jamais rien vu, le monde eût été fermé pour moi, car la vie extérieure semble avoir été faite pour l'homme et non pour la femme. Cependant j'aime à me plonger dans le bain de la vie populaire, à sentir les ondes de la foule couler sur moi, à m'imprégner des fluides du peuple. Ainsi seulement je possède une ville et j'en sais ce que le touriste ne comprendra jamais, malgré toutes les explications de ses guides.] (73)

This passage makes apparent the split in Eberhardt's gender identification: while her use of water imagery—for example, "j'aime à me plonger dans le bain ... à m'imprégner des fluides"—defines her writing as "feminine."[13] The specular metaphor of vision, her voyeuristic desire to observe the "popular life," and her urge to "possess" a city all point to her identification with a phallocentric discursive position that would cater to the colonialist desire for mastery. In the context of her colonial encounter, this statement about her cross-dressing seems more suggestive of her identification with the male discourse of Orientalism. Although she is correct about the limitations her gender imposed on her life, Eberhardt's rationalization of her male persona, as a logistic necessity, is indicative of the orientalist's desire to penetrate the inaccessible layers of Oriental society and possess the "real" signifiers of Oriental culture from which the ordinary tourist is excluded. Eberhardt clearly distinguishes herself from the European tourist by claiming a certain will to knowledge and discovery characteristic of male colonialist travelers. For her, cross-dressing was a disguise that gave her access to what she could not otherwise obtain as a European woman in the Orient. Transvestism is here viewed not as a mode of identification with the Other but as a kind of phallocentric appropriation of the Oriental signifiers—parasitic now of the Orient itself—behind which her European self always prevails. Eberhardt's adoption of male oriental garment in this instance is therefore a form of colonial mimicry—or "going native"—that reaffirms the essential difference between the colonizer and the colonized and is thus consistent with the logic of colonialist discourse.[14] In this sense, transvestism is not a space of possibility that challenges categories of race and gender, as Garber claims, but an appropriation of the third category to reaffirm the binary logic that separates the colonizer from the colonized, the European woman from the Oriental man.

And yet, as an affirmative articulation of the difference between Oriental appearance and European essence, orientalist transvestism can and did in the case of Eberhardt produce the effect of identification with the Other: "enveloping" oneself in the Other's clothes, as I have suggested in previous chapters, implies and imposes the desire to occupy the place of the Other, a "transcultural" urge to become a "real" Oriental through cross-dressing.[15] In her first diary, Eberhardt provides an alternative view of her cross-dressing: "At this moment, rather like the rest of my life, I have but one desire: to don [revêtir], as soon as possible, the favorite identity [la personnalité aimée] which, in reality, is my true one [la vraie], and return there, to Africa, and pick up that life [i.e., the life of vagabondage] ... sleep, in the coolness and profound silence, under the breathtaking fall of the

stars, with the infinite sky as my roof and the warm ground for my bed"
(304).

This passage too is characteristic of Eberhardt's ambivalence toward her
cross-dressing in that both sides of her identity seem alternatively to be
her "true" self. Here, Eberhardt makes no distinction between appearance and essence, as the boundaries between vestimentary reality and
psychic reality blur. Her wish to return to her "*personnalité aimée*" is a clear
reference to her adopted identity as Si Mahmoud Saadi, the young Arab
scholar, whom she considers her "real" self. The slippage between her
costume and her race and gender identity apparent in her use of the verb
revêtir in this context and her emphasis on the word *vraie* are indicative of
her identification with her masculine appearance. She wants to "put on"
again her Oriental identity just like a garment that designates the truth of
what lies beneath. Eberhardt's transvestism thus seems to have constituted the path for a transformation of identity, allowing her to rewrite her
subjectivity from that of a European woman to that of an Oriental man.
This is also reaffirmed in her use of masculine adjectives in referring to
herself in her writing.

As the site of a double negation—of both her femininity and her Europeanness—Eberhardt's adoption of male Oriental identity was crucial to
her self-fashioning as a split orientalist subject. Her transvestism provided
her, above all, with the possibility of transcending the sociocultural limitations of her gender,[16] which was necessary to her survival in such a male-
dominated field as Orientalism as well as in the Orient itself: "As I distance
myself from the limbos of the past [i.e., her life as a woman], my character
forms and asserts itself exactly as I wished. What grows in me [ce qui
se développe en moi] is a most unrelenting and invincible energy and
straightforwardness of the heart, two qualities that I value more than any
other, and alas, so rare among women. With that, and four months of
living in the desert, most probably this Spring, I am sure to become
someone" (308).

Transvestism for Eberhardt was not merely a performative gesture, it
was constructive of a new gender identity. In adopting a male persona she
claimed to have actually developed certain character traits culturally at-
tributed to men, a claim that suggests that cross-dressing for Eberhardt
was not so much a blurring of distinctions as it was a desire to have a
different gender. In other words, she was not so much calling into question the binary logic of gender as she was identifying with the male persona. Her use of the intransitive verb *se développer* suggests her belief in a

psychic transfiguration through transvestism, which seems to have endowed her with the opinionated energy and "emotional" uprightness that
she thought she lacked as a woman. Orientalist transvestism thus involves
an identification with male desire and a denial of "femininity" that is
articulated in orientalist discourse as a lack, a lack that must be overcome
in "becoming someone"—a reference to her desire to be a great orientalist writer.[17] Cross-dressing, in short, is a way of obeying the patriarchal law
that underpins colonialist relations of power—the feminization of the
Orient by the West.

But Eberhardt's cultural cross-dressing as an Oriental also involved a
displacement of her European culture, which she considered crucial for
her "*développement.*" Her goal in traveling in North Africa was not only to be
"far from the profane banalities of the invading West," as an escapist
traveler, but also to have an opportunity, as a believer of "transculturation," to "inspire [herself] with the great evocative ideas of Islamic faith,
which is the peace of the soul" (68, 69). She achieved this spiritual aspect
of her subjective transformation by staying in different *zaouïyas* (the religious schools of confraternities)—from which women were excluded.
Here she tried to acquire the profound and personal understanding of
Islamic culture and spirituality she considered necessary to living in a
Moslem society: "To live with these cloistered and susceptible men, it is
necessary to have penetrated their ideas, to have made these ideas one's
own, to have purified them by forcing them to go back to their ancient
source" (121). Although this statement has an orientalist undertone apparent in her wish to "penetrate" the Other's field of knowledge, it does
nonetheless point to her cross-religious identification, and thus expresses
her desire to go beyond the orientalist imaginary and become a "true"
Oriental through a full adoption of Islamic ideas. Eberhardt's ambivalence
enabled her to view her colonial encounter as a two-way street, providing
the possibility of an "other" self-fashioning through what the local culture
had to offer. For her, orientalist transvestism constituted the possibility of
a cultural transformation through which she became an introspective
subject in the Other's symbolic.

Transvestism and the Colonial Encounter

Eberhardt's unique position as an orientalist transvestite profoundly fixated on Oriental culture made her both a threat to colonial power and a
useful instrument to be recuperated by its informational apparatus. For

transvestism, I have been arguing, is a split phenomenon, caught between the economies of desire and power, law and transgression. On the one hand, Eberhardt's desire for the Orient had subversive potential, as her immersion in Oriental culture made her both a political rebel and a literary dissident—not to mention her transgressive cross-dressing, which was subversive in relation to both gender and racial categories of French colonialism. From the time of her first journey to the Tunisian coast, her encounter with the reality of the French Empire had provoked in her a profound sense of resentment against colonialism, so that this passionate orientalist participated, for example, in the Muslim student revolt against the French Empire in the spring of 1899, and later in the activities of the Qadriya confraternity, a site of native political opposition. But beyond such blunt acts of resistance, which led to her expulsion from Algeria in the spring of 1901, Eberhardt's conversion to Islam and her friendship with local people went against the grain of colonial relations of power, while her cross-dressing surely problematized the gender boundaries crucial in the construction of colonial authority—the colonizer as the "powerful man," and the Oriental as the effeminate Other. Her identification with Orientals, her cultural assimilation, conceivably disturbed colonial identity based on a discriminatory mode of racial differentiation: the desire for the Orient inevitably implies disavowal of the colonizer's claim to racial superiority.

In conjunction with her political activism, Eberhardt's writing as the site of a discursive ambivalence marks a conscious deviation from the norms of official Orientalism. One may call her writing a "transvestite writing," a mode of articulation that blurs the boundaries of representer and represented, orientalist and Oriental. While her discourse of discontent undermines the ethnocentrism of the European savant, her sympathetic representations of the Maghreb problematize the stereotypical images of the Orient that give the discriminatory power of colonialism its currency. As a split writer, Eberhardt produced the limit-text of Orientalism where the repressed voice of its discontent exposes the ideological shortcomings of the dominant discourse. Eberhardt was, I have been suggesting, the figuration of noise in the discursive system of Orientalism, a dissident in relation to colonialism's modes of representation; her writing was the static in the communication system.

And yet, to the extent that desire for the Orient is mediated by the orientalist desire for knowledge, Eberhardt's subversive self-orientalization had the potential of being recuperated by the system it opposed. Just as the orientalist parasite lives on the colonial order while producing noise in its discursive system, so is colonial power able to "parasite" the orientalist's subversive desire to produce a new order. There is, in other words, a circular relation between the system and its noise, order and disorder, power and its effect of desire. Once within a parasitic relation, the orientalist cannot avoid being parasitized because in such a relation no position is ontologically fixed—but, I want to insist, the system that parasitizes her cannot avoid being changed in turn by its recuperation of noise. To illustrate the circular—or, more accurately, spiralling—structure of orientalist parasitism, I turn to Eberhardt's relation with Victor Barrucand, the editor of the colonial magazine *El Akhbar*, and General Hubert Lyautey, commander of the French troops in Aïn-Sefra from 1903, after she returned to Algeria in the winter of 1902.

Eberhardt's marriage to a young Spahi, Slimène Ehnni, in October 1901 gave her French citizenship and enabled her, in an ironic twist, to come back to Algeria, where she spent the rest of her life. Here she met Barrucand, who took a keen interest in her work and decided to use her as a collaborator for *El Akhbar*—a bilingual magazine in the service of the colonialist policy intended to "serve France in her natural inclination toward justice and racial equality, avoiding the excesses of the arabophiles as much as of the arabophobes."[18] Eberhardt's mastery of vernacular Arabic and her broad knowledge of local tribes and Islamic culture made her a valuable resource for the information-gathering apparatus of French colonialism. In the fall of 1903, Barrucand, attentive to the need for information to aid the colonial expansion of France into the southwest region of Algeria, sent Isabelle to the Sud-Oranais to report on the French army's "pacification" of "insurgent" tribes. Eberhardt, driven by her insatiable desire for adventure and her "fundamental need," as she herself claimed, for "a change in scenery," traveled twice to the Sud-Oranais and produced a rich autobiographical ethnography of the indigenous tribes who were being invaded by the French army (412). The two-part text—which was saved by the "unrelenting will" of Lyautey, who sent his soldiers to recover it from the rubble of Isabelle's house after a flood killed her—was given to Barrucand to be edited for publication as "Dans l'ombre chaude de l'Islam" in 1906.

This collection of journalistic reports takes the form of a discursive drift much like Isabelle's journey in search of "the profound voluptuousness of wandering life" (126). Like Flaubert's *Notes de voyages*, Eberhardt's *Sud-Oranais* is a heterogeneous text, split by its ambivalent subject and dispersed as a result of her varied interests. Her report alternates between long and repetitious accounts of the strategies of the French troops in the region and short sketches including ethnographic representations of the indigenous people and anecdotes of her relationships with them. As a modern orientalist text, it depends for its narrative economy on a principle of discontinuity that allows the emergence of a whole series of descriptive statements belonging to different epistemological domains and producing a kind of encyclopedic corpus of information about the region.

But this participation in the colonial activity of information collecting is a suggestive illustration of the relation between colonial power and the desire for the Orient. Consider, for example, the very beginning of the Sud-Oranais where Isabelle explains her motivations for pursuing such an arduous journey: "A heavy ennui weighed down on Algiers, and I let myself go into a hazy inertia without pleasure and without sorrow, and which, without desires either, could have had the sweetness of annihilation. All of a sudden the battle of El-Moungar broke out, and with it, the possibility of seeing the harsh regions of the South again: I went to Sud-Oranais, as reporter . . . the dream of so many months was going to be realized, and so suddenly" (125). Eberhardt's desire for the journey has its roots in an "ennui" that recalls the motivation of her earlier journey along the Tunisian coast, in which she participated in colonial tax gathering. Like her participation in collecting tax from the natives, information collecting is here represented as an opportunity to indulge in a pleasurable tour of exoticism. The desire for the Orient, in other words, is not exterior to the relations of colonial power. Rather, it is a formative element, a seductive feature on which the power that produces it is predicated. The discourse of Orientalism embodies a place for its practitioner's desire, a crucial principle that underlies the recuperative power of colonialism. Isabelle often describes in her narrative the "joy . . . of watching in peace the day end in red glow on the simplicity of things," and the pleasant experience of the "new scenery" with its "impression of the immobility of beings and things," experiences that allowed her to endure the difficulties of the war-stricken region and continue to accomplish her colonial task of information collecting (126, 237, 269).

Eberhardt found in her new task of colonial reporting an ideal place for the realization of her desire to frequent zaouïyas—as Si Mahmoud, the young Arab scholar in search of Koranic knowledge. Zaouïyas were suspected of being loci of Muslim opposition against the French expansion

into the border region. The colonial system, aware that Eberhardt's transvestism enabled her to "go everywhere undetected," used her as an unin-
tentional colonial agent (240). Eberhardt's involvement with *zaouïyas* was
an ideal situation of mutual parasitism: while she benefited from the
colonial system by indulging in her own desire to immerse herself in
Islamic culture and play out her male identity, the colonial information
apparatus used her to gain information about the strongholds of native
opposition. In such a circular relation of appropriation, desire and power
produce each other as their effects. Here the exercise of colonial power
acts as an instrument of derived satisfaction while desire is reinscribed in
the relations of colonial power as a mode of surveillance.

But if Eberhardt's desire for the Orient became an instrument of power,
it was not always to produce "valuable" information. She generated noise
as well. In fact, her writing during her Sud-Oranais journey often entails
more noise than "valuable" information. In spite of her role as a colonial
reporter, her writings are fraught with cacophonous messages that are
usually discordant with the strategic needs of the colonial system of communication. Eberhardt's reports on the Ziania confraternity in Kenadsa
during her second trip to Sud-Oranais are a case in point.

Lyautey's infamous "heart and mind" strategy—*tache d'huile*, as it was
called—for taking over the southern regions of Doui-Ménia and the
Ouled-Djérir in 1903 depended on the friendly cooperation of Sidi Brahim
Ould Mohammed, the head of the Ziania confraternity, who had given
mixed messages to the general about his commitment to a peaceful com-
promise. In a shrewd strategic move to learn more about the political
views of this religious institution, General Lyautey, who had met Isabelle a
couple of months earlier and knew about her initiation into Qadriya
brotherhood and about her friendship with a famous female marabout,
Lella Zeyneb, asked her to visit the confraternity. Once again, both sides
profited from the encounter: Isabelle in her search for Islamic spirituality
and the French army in its pursuit of information to be used for a complete takeover.

Eberhardt's copious writings during her sojourn at Ziania constitute a
"noisy channel" of communication because they usually recount her own
search for pleasure and internal peace as opposed to strategic information
about the confraternity. On her arrival, for example, she is overwhelmed
by the serene atmosphere of the *zaouïya*: "A thought of good Nirvana
already softens my heart: the desert which I crossed was that of my desires. When my will shall awaken, it seems that it will want new things and

that I will no longer remember anything about my past sufferings. I dream of a sleep that would be a death, and from which one would emerge armed with an invigorated personality, regenerated and strong by forgetfulness, and requenched in unconsciousness" (246). Far from being the report of a secret agent, this passage reflects Eberhardt's profound death drive and her escapist desire to immerse herself in the spiritual setting and allow herself to be regenerated by the unconscious, by oblivion. The colonial agency here has obviously produced a locus of desire where the spy is transformed into a spiritual seeker, participating in mystical activities while producing an irrelevant "message" rather than information. Instead of acting as a secret agent, she identifies with—or even assimilates into, as Laura Rice suggests—the Islamic culture and thus becomes a happy associate in the scouted institution to the point that she becomes nostalgic about leaving it. In her melancholic reflections during her last night at the zaouïya, she explains how she has used her distance from the crowd of colonizers to achieve a "feeling of blessed rest," a sentiment that brings to focus Isabelle's disidentification with colonialism's apparatus of power (277). As a discourse of desire, Eberhardt's reflections thus seem to elude the colonial power relations in this instance, for she clearly used them for her personal benefit: as an orientalist parasite, she lived off both the colonial system and the Oriental society and produced no valuable information in exchange.

The noise produced by the orientalist parasite disturbs the colonial order, but in its function of disorder, I argue, it catalyzes a new and more complex order. As the complicitous mediator of the colonial relation, Eberhardt's writings engendered the possibility of a shift from assimilation to association in French colonial policy.[19] The invasion of southwestern Algeria was the product of the old doctrine of assimilation that advocated a complete integration of the Other in a unified colonial administration. As a centralized policy of rattachement, and heavily informed by militarism, it meant a forceful invasion of territories to secure an almost noncontiguous colony and force the native population to adopt French culture—or "learn" the putative wisdom of French culture. Eberhardt's observations in the Ziania confraternity and among the nomad tribes clearly ran counter to this kind of colonial order and seem to have advocated a more flexible, decentralized attitude toward the region. In "Choses du Sud Oranais," she rejects the unsuccessful attempts of the French army in their aggressive expeditions against the Ksourien tribes and the violent extermination of the nomads. Her reports from Sud-

Oranais made it clear to Lyautey and his associates that "it is useless to fight against profound and insurmountable causes and that a lasting transposition of civilization is not possible" (296). Eberhardt's strong critique of the French doctrine of assimilation and her own associative relation with the Ziania marabouts and with native tribesmen seem to have convinced Lyautey that the more humane and efficient policy of association would be more appropriate in dealing with the Sud-Oranais.

As a young colonizer interested in North African culture and pragmatic about the colonial rule, Lyautey was already a strong supporter of the new idea of association presented by the French colonial lobby, which aimed at a more indirect, flexible rule that would gain native cooperation. Although I want to avoid hyperbolizing Eberhardt's influence on Lyautey, their friendship during her stay in the Sud-Oranais seems to have played a crucial role in Lyautey's final adoption of association in dealing with the nomadic tribes and his decision to avoid a complete invasion of the region. It is difficult to speculate about how Lyautey read Eberhardt's mystical discourse, but it seems that her spiritualism functioned as an interfering message that made the colonial general aware of how respect for the Other—expressed as a desire for the Orient in Eberhardt—could be put to use as a "milder, gentler" means of control. Eberhardt's writings posited a theoretical field in which to reconsider the inadequacies of the assimilation policy, while her associative relation with the Orientals provided a paradigm for the practice of the new order. Her account of her stay in the Ziania zaouïya encouraged Lyautey to relinquish his violent and ineffectual attacks against the native population and use negotiation, or "associative" friendship, as a strategy to deal with the border dispute. Eberhardt thus played the differential role of a catalyst whose parasitism within the colonial system mediated the shift from a detailed program of absolute domination to a general policy of more subtle control. Eberhardt's writing is an odd point in the network of colonial discourse, which, by producing an effect of noise and disorder, subtly helped to transform the colonial strategies of domination.

Eberhardt's mediating role in the shift from assimilation to association is important to understanding colonialism because it makes evident the mediated structure of colonial rule. Colonialism has often been viewed as a stable practice of domination exercised through a static binary relation between the colonizer and the colonized. Eberhardt's parasitic role in North Africa problematizes such simple notions of colonial power and attests to the complex versatility of its structure. Because it is in mediated relation with its object, colonialism is a discontinuous exercise of power whose strategies are neither uniform nor stable. In fact, what makes its functioning efficient is precisely its mobile and fluid character, which enables it to recuperate and use points of opposition in its transformations. Eberhardt's involvement in the colonial relation thus made it necessary to reconsider oppositionality as a negative force in relation to power and to view it, more accurately, as a productive element for colonial power in its processes of restructuring and reform, as a useful instrument to produce more efficient relations of power—more efficient precisely because they were better adjusted toward and more tolerable to those on whom they were exercised.

"Tristesse du Depart": An Open-ended Conclusion

❂

While I was struggling to find a way to conclude this work on belated Orientalism, feeling, like modern orientalists, at once melancholy about writing my "last words" of the "journey" and utterly wary of committing the sin of closure—what Flaubert acutely called *bêtise*—a friend showed me a recent orientalist catalog from Tweeds Clothing Company which provided me with an interesting context in which to reconsider the sociocultural implications of what I have said about Orientalism. Ironically, this catalog constructs its theme of traveling to Egypt as a postmodern version of Flaubert's journey, claiming pretentiously to embark on a similar voyage of discovery more than a century later. The glamorous photos of attractive models posing against the "exotic" Egyptian landscape are accompanied by captions made of decontextualized quotations from Flaubert's travel notes to produce the effects of authenticity and originality.

This orientalist catalog, as part of a whole range of what Renato Rosaldo calls "imperialist nostalgia," is a disturbing reminder that the discourse of exoticism is alive and well today.[1] It is indeed startling to see that despite the postcolonial critiques of Orientalism as well as the recent "multicultural" *prise de conscience*, the Orient's imaginative space is still being appropriated as a decorative foil. Indeed, the current "embracing" of alterity seems, ironically, to have actually abetted the recent reemergence of imperial nostalgia, a phenomenon that ought to caution us against premature celebration of our "postcolonial victories."

Tweeds's rediscovery of Egypt through Flaubert's writing is emblematic of how an earlier "discourse of discontent" can be appropriated to perpetuate orientalist stereotypes. To be sure, Flaubert's aesthetic discourse is used primarily as a marketing strategy to transform an otherwise ordinary form of advertisement into a seemingly "sophisticated" discourse of exploration that is more effective in selling clothes to fashionable yuppies, a trend that has recently become widespread in fashion magazines such as *Elle, Harper's Bazaar,* and *Details.* The decontextualized quotations from Flaubert's travel notes—such as "this is a great place for contrasts"—are used to *authorize* the catalog's orientalist quest for exotic signifiers that incite the reader to look "different" by purchasing Tweeds's clothing. The text of a "discontented" orientalist, in other words, produces a desire for the Orient through which the clothing company can sell its clothing more efficiently. But such a capitalistic usage empties Flaubert's text of its oppositional tendencies and utilizes it as an affirmative discourse of exoticism that reinforces the stereotypes of Oriental otherness. Flaubert's ambivalent discourse here becomes the *authoritative* intertext through whose mediating function Tweeds's catalog can "legitimately" repeat trite representations of Oriental culture.

Tweeds's orientalist catalog testifies to the strength of the imperialist fantasies that continue to inform the dialectic of self and Other in our postcolonial era. The catalog's introductory statement bluntly claims, "We did not want our journey to be filled with snapshots of an antique land. Instead we wanted to rediscover our clothing in the context of a different culture." The Orient's "exotic" image repertoire, that "bewildering chaos of colours," functions here again as a differential sign of otherness against which a company like Tweeds can display its colorful clothing. That orientalist exoticism and colonial nostalgia help Tweeds and other companies sell their clothing demonstrates the desirability of such fantasies in the West today, fantasies that can also be implicated in such neocolonial interventions as the Gulf War. Exotic images of the Orient coupled with ethnocentric representations of the Islamic world as a locus of terrorism and fanaticism continue to extend colonial violence into the neocolonial era.

That Orientalism has maintained its dominant ideological force to this day through its productive and recuperative strategies ought to caution one against theorizing ambivalent discursive practices solely in terms of discontinuity and opposition. Throughout my discussion of belated Orientalism I have emphasized its dispersive tactics, discursive heterogeneities, strategic irregularities, and historical discontinuities. I have tried to show how such texts as Nerval's *Voyage en Orient* and Flaubert's *Notes de voyages* inscribe themselves as crucial points of opposition in the power relations of the dominant discourse. I have attempted to theorize their deviations and modes of differentiation to problematize the monolithic

notion of Orientalism's internal "coherence" and to account for its transformations. But what about continuity, repetition, and return, the elements and modalities that remain the same throughout Orientalism's
modern history? Does not Orientalism's ideological dominance in this
postcolonial era testify to the internal "coherence" of its discursive field?
Should one, therefore, not study the discontinuities of counterdiscursive
practices in relation to their productive strategies of propagation?

These are questions that readers may have about my discussion of
Orientalism. Although at several points—for example, in delineating the
discursive shift from the travelogue to the tourist guide, or in defining the
desire for the Orient in relation to orientalist desire—I attempt to account
for the phenomena of repetition and continuity, I have not stressed (as
other critics have) the discursive regularities and strategic congruities in
orientalist representations. Instead, my aim has been to account for the
proliferation of orientalist representation through the enabling effects of
discontinuity and difference. Orientalism, to borrow a phrase from Serres,
works because it doesn't work. Discursive slippage and disorientation are
catalysts in orientalist epistemology and colonialist power; they mediate
new rules of formation that cater to changing conditions in the relation
between the West and its Others. The phenomena of repetition and continuity thus should not lead us to conclude that Orientalism is a coherent
and unified body of knowledge, for it is precisely Orientalism's ambivalence and discursive discontinuities that help it to maintain an ideologically consistent discourse of domination. Perhaps one ought to theorize,
in even greater detail, Orientalism's capacity to maintain its will to power
on the basis of the representational irregularities and discursive disorder
that I have discussed in this text. How and at what points is a counterdiscourse recuperated by the dominant discourses? What kinds of changes
occur in the orientalist-colonialist relations of power once an oppositional tendency is co-opted?

I have tried to suggest throughout this book about belated Orientalism
that split discursive practices should not necessarily be viewed as negative
forces in the relations of power. More accurately, they should be considered formative elements through whose mediated role that dominant
discourse maintains its cultural hegemony. I have tried to avoid dichoto-
mizing the relations of power and the desire for the Orient by emphasiz-
ing the *relational* character of the orientalist formation. Following Bhabha's
provocative observation that "hybridity is the sign of the productivity of
colonial power,"[2] I have intimated that the effect of splitting reimplicates

the desire for the Orient in strategies of domination and control. But it remains to describe even further the specificities of how the relations of power are enacted on the site of this desire through the articulation of ambivalence. And it will be necessary in further work to discuss more extensively Orientalism's circulatory system of discursive exchange in which desire and power produce one another. Mapping this complex relation will require an even more detailed historical study of split Orientalism in which aesthetic representations of the Orient are analyzed in their dynamic relationship with the administrative and institutional discourses. Further study may account for the ways the aesthetic representations and their oppositional tendencies are produced and appropriated within the larger history of other sociocultural productions.

No less important is the need to specify in the site of what I have called generally "the desire for the Orient." Clearly, complex political, social, cultural, and psychological factors are at work in producing the desire for the Orient within the network of Orientalism's power relations, and this book has attempted to delineate some of these factors. I have discussed the desire for the Orient in the mid-nineteenth century in its mediated relation to the orientalist desire for knowledge and mastery, whose genealogical roots I locate in the discourse of late eighteenth-century Orientalism. But the mediated production of the desire for the Orient needs to be studied not purely as an *intertextual* phenomenon but rather as a *social* phenomenon inscribed in a variety of everyday practices, practices that cannot be reified into a single theoretical system whose totalizing impulse leaves little room for historical specificity.[3] Foucault is to the point in rejecting the modalities of the "universal" and the "general" and "calling for a new mode of the connection between theory and practice." This new mode, he argues persuasively, ought to "conduct an ascending analysis of power, starting, that is, from its infinitesimal mechanisms, which each have their own history, their own trajectory, . . . and then see how these mechanisms of power have been—and continue to be—invested, colonised, utilised, . . . by forms of global domination."[4] The kind of research project that *Belated Travelers* describes belongs to this category of historiography: I have attempted to demonstrate the importance of micromechanisms of the discourse of colonial power and to explain how an understanding of their articulation problematizes descending analyses of the orientalist encounter which misconstrue it as a general phenomenon of monolithic domination. New studies of Orientalism must delve even deeper into the sociocultural particularities of its production and its variant manifestations in different historical contexts. One might consider, for example, to what extent modern orientalists' desire for the Orient is mediated and inspired by the phenomenon of *turquerie* in clothing fashion, or by the orientalist plays and operas they see. The question may also be posed as to how the relations of orientalist power and desire are produced within and through ordinary activities of everyday life.

My aim in pointing out some of these new theoretical directions and the critical lacunae in my own study of belated Orientalism is not merely to acknowledge what I have failed to accomplish. Nor is it a deceptive attempt to avoid dealing with unresolved issues pertinent to making my argument. Rather, my goal is to emphasize the need for an open-ended discussion of Orientalism as a tactic of critical opposition to the recuperative strategies of dominant discourses. In an interview republished in *The Post-colonial Critic*, Gayatri Spivak mentions cleaning or brushing one's teeth as an analogy to describe what she calls "the practical politics of the open end."[5] Such activities as brushing one's teeth or exercising are done in a spirit of daily maintenance, unlike a surgical operation, they do not bring about a drastic transformation. Viewed as such obviates being pessimistic about "fighting a losing battle against morality" or remaining idealistic about the outcome of these activities—the fact is that "all these efforts are doomed to failure because we are going to die" (105). In an open-ended political practice, both of these extreme tendencies, pessimism and idealism, are at work, "each bringing the other to [a productive] crisis." The practical politics of the open end, Spivak remarks, "is not like some kind of massive ideological act (the surgical operation) which brings about a drastic change."[6]

An effective critique of Orientalism must view itself as an interminable struggle and a perpetually revisionist project that constantly questions its theoretical assumptions and reconsiders its critical tactics. Since the power relations involved in representations of the Other are themselves in a continual process of transformation and restructuration that ensures discourse of power its cultural hegemony, no definite political program of critical practice is adequate in problematizing effectively the limits of orientalist representations. One can only engage in a shifting and indeterminate practice of deconstruction, describing the ideological complexities and political strategies of Orientalism in order to expose their limitations and problems. An open-ended political practice, therefore, should avoid the trap of theoretical orthodoxy by continually reevaluating its mode of criticism and reexamining the implications of its oppositional tactics while maintaining an unremitting challenge to racial, ideological, and imperialist stereotypes. New studies of the colonial encounter are not merely derivative exercises; they are also crucial and necessary interventionist practices that question both the tokenizing idea that earlier critics have already covered everything that needs to be said about the historical predicament of colonialism and the orthodox tendency to reiterate previous critical positions.

Finally, because no critic can occupy a sociocultural position "outside" the relations of power, and because she or he has only a partial perspective of the political field, practitioners of open-ended criticism need to inquire into the implications of their own critical predicaments. In recent postcolonial discourses there has been a tendency to displace and contain one's own cultural and institutional situation by foregrounding the politics of representation in the colonial past, evading any discussion of the ways the "I" is implicated in relations of power. To avoid a new mode of critical transcendentalism, the conjunctural position of the speaking subject has to be figured into his or her discourse.[7] Throughout my study of Orientalism, I have been haunted by a question: Am I a postcolonial orientalist because I research and write about European representations of the Orient within the institutional space of the "Western" academy? To the extent that my postcolonial discourse on Orientalism has been produced within the institutional and discursive formation of the West, I must acknowledge, melancholically, that it remains within the field of orientalist power relations. Nevertheless, my work can, I hope, contribute fragments to that "profound meditation on the myths of western power and knowledge which confine the colonized and dispossessed to a half-life of misrepresentation and migration."[8] For a work such as this belongs to an anamnesiac order, working against the kinds of cultural amnesia that circumvent the question of history and thus perpetuate systems of neocolonial oppression.

Notes

❀

Unless otherwise stated, all translations of French quotations are mine.

Introduction: The Predicaments of Belatedness

1 Cf. Edward Said, "Traveling Theory," in *The World, the Text, and the Critic* (Cambridge: Harvard University Press, 1983).

2 James Clifford, "Notes on Theory and Travel," *Inscriptions* 5 (1989):177.

3 Louis Althusser, *Lenin and Philosophy and Other Essays*, trans. Ben Brester (London: NLB, 1971).

4 Edward Said, "Opponents, Audiences, Constituencies and Community," in *The Anti-Aesthetic: Essays on Postmodern Culture*, ed. Hal Foster (Port Townsend, Wash.: Bay Press, 1983), 140–41.

5 This irony is most evident in the case of Dinesh D'Sousa, who, having served as a White House domestic policy analyst, argues against the politics of race and sex on campus.

6 Said, "Opponents, Audiences, Constituencies and Community," 157.

7 Edward Said, *Orientalism* (New York: Vintage Books, 1978).

8 Homi Bhabha, "The Other Question: Difference, Discrimination and the Discourse of Colonialism," in *Literature, Politics, and Theory*, ed. Francis Barker et al. (London: Methuen, 1986), 149; my emphasis.

9 Said, "Orientalism Reconsidered," in Barker et al., ibid., 216. Ironically, Said himself ignores this history in *Orientalism*, a crucial problem which Said attempts to remedy in his new book, *Culture and Imperialism* (New York: Alfred A. Knopf, 1993) by devoting a whole section to "Resistance and Opposition."

10 Needless to say, many postcolonial readers have made and continue to make cultural critiques of current neocolonial practices, but even these critics invoke colonial memory in constructing their oppositional identities.

11 Johannes Fabian, *Time and the Other: How Anthropology Makes Its Object* (New York: Columbia University Press, 1983).

12 Malek Alloula, *The Colonial Harem*, trans. Myrna Godzich and Wald Godzich (Minneapolis: University of Minnesota Press, 1986), 4–5; my emphasis.

13 Sander Gilman, "Black Bodies, White Bodies: Toward an Iconography of Female Sexuality in Late Nineteenth-Century Art, Medicine, and Literature," in *"Race," Writing, and Difference*, ed. Henry Louis Gates, Jr. (Chicago: University of Chicago Press, 1985).

14 Michel Foucault, *Power/Knowledge*, ed. Colin Gordon (New York: Pantheon Books, 1972), 83.

15 James Clifford has pointed out in his interesting essay on Said's *Orientalism* that the genealogical limitations of Said's "tendentious approach"—i.e., the exclusive emphasis on the Arab Middle East and the elimination of German Orientalism—have the potential to undermine the rigor of his critique. See "On Orientalism," in *The Predicament of Culture* (Cambridge: Harvard University Press, 1988), 225–76.

16 This is a criticism made also by Lisa Lowe in her *Critical Terrains: French and British Orientalisms* (Ithaca: Cornell University Press, 1991), in which she rejects Said's "totalizing framework" and argues for "the heterogeneity of the orientalist object, whose contradictions and lack of fixity mark precisely the moments of instability in the discourse" (x). My project, like hers, does not view the European discourse on the Other as a "single developmental tradition" but treats it instead as a complex field of heterogeneous practices marked by a plurality of interests and critical formations. My argument, however, is more historically and polemically specific than hers. While *Critical Terrains* covers three centuries of orientalist discourse in four chapters, this volume addresses the specific historical conditions of late nineteenth-century Orientalism implicated in both the economies of desire and power, a split that produces a moment of discontinuity in the colonial episteme. Also, my argument about the heterogeneity of Orientalism, as it will become evident throughout my discussions, is meant to demonstrate the ways in which the discourse of power depends on discontinuity and specification to produce new sites of authority. In this sense, heterogeneity is an enabling force in the production and transformation of colonial power, one that ensures its currency in new historical conjunctures.

17 Bhabha, "The Other Question," 158. This argument is also made by Achille Mbembe in a more detailed and concrete discussion of (post)colonial power; see "The Banality of Power and the Aesthetics of Vulgarity in the Postcolony," *Public Culture* 4.2 (Spring 1992):1–30.

18 Aijaz Ahmad, *In Theory: Classes, Nations, Literatures* (London: Verso, 1992), 166.

19 Cf. Michel Foucault, *La Volonté de savoir* (Paris: Gallimard, 1976); *Surveiller et punir: Naissance de la prison* (Paris: Gallimard, 1975), 30–34.

20 Cf. Chris Bongie, *Exotic Memories: Literature, Colonialism, and the Fin de Siècle* (Stanford: Stanford University Press, 1991).

1. Orientalist Desire, Desire for the Orient:
Ideological Splits in Nerval

1   See, for example, Ross Chambers, *Gérard de Nerval et La poétique du voyage* (Paris: Corti, 1969), 223–68; Michel Jeanneret, Introduction to Nerval's *Voyage en Orient* (Paris: Garnier-Flammarion, 1980), 38–41; Gérard Schaeffer, *Le Voyage en Orient de Nerval. Etudes des structures* (Neuchâtel: La Baconnière, 1967).

2   Lacan uses this German term to indicate the division of the subject between the unconscious self and the conscious subject of discourse. See, in particular, "Fonction et champ de la parole et du langage en psychanalyse," in his *Écrits* (Paris: Editions du Seuil, 1971). Following Lacan's discussion of the subject's inauguration into the symbolic field of discourse, I will show how official Orientalism, like the symbolic function, mediates and organizes the orientalist's relation to the Orient in his or her accession to the field of its discursive practice.

3   Said, *Orientalism*, 182.

4   Chateaubriand, *Itinéraire de Paris à Jérusalem*, ed. Jean Mourot (Paris: Garnier-Flammarion, 1968), 41.

5   Constantin de Volney, *Voyage en Egypte et en Syrie*, ed. Jean Gaulmier (Paris: Mouton, 1959), 22.

6   To speak of personal involvement as a more "positive" mode of relating to the Oriental experience, however, does not suggest that it is free of ideological limitations of Orientalism. On the contrary, such an experience bodies forth a "philosophy of presence" and a mode of self-identification that implicate it in relations of power.

7   Michel Butor, "Le voyage et l'écriture," in *Répertoire IV* (Paris: Editions de Minuit, 1971), 25.

8   Gérard de Nerval, *Le Voyage en Orient*, 2 vols., ed. Michel Jeanneret (Paris: Garnier-Flammarion, 1980), 1:149. All page references hereafter are given parenthetically in the text.

9   Volney, *Voyage en Egypte et en Syrie*, 23.

10   Jean-Marie Carré makes a similar point about Nerval's style of journey in his *Voyageurs et écrivains français en Egypte* (Cairo: Imprimerie de l'Institut Français d'Archéologie Orientale, 1956); he describes Nerval as both a "genuine reporter who undertakes an exploratory voyage," and a "gentle flâneur, a gracious fool who leaves with a stroke of inspiration" [doux flâneur, un gentil fol qui s'en va au hasard de l'inspiration] (2:9).

11   For a short discussion of the distinction I am making here between representation and figuration, see Roland Barthes, *Le plaisir du texte* (Paris: Points-Editions du Seuil, 1973), 88–90.

12   An interesting article by Andreas Wetzel, "Décrire L'Espagne: référent et réalité dans le récit de voyage littéraire," *Stanford French Review* 11.3 (Fall 1987):359–73, shows how a travelogue borrows its truth from intertextual references despite its

claim to represent the immediate reality as seen by the traveler. Edward Said makes a similar point in *Orientalism* when he says that "the Orient is less a place than a *topos*, a set of references, a congeries of characteristics, that seems to have its origin in a quotation, or a fragment of a text, or a citation from someone's work on the Orient, or some bit of previous imagining, or an amalgam of all these" (177).

13   Jeanneret, Introduction to Nerval, *Voyage en Orient*, 1:22–23.

14   In *Three Essays on Theory of Sexuality*, trans. James Strachey (New York: Basic Books, 1962), Freud shows the necessary relation between concealment of the body and sexual desire, arguing that "the progressive concealment of the body which goes with civilization keeps sexual curiosity awake" (22). But Nerval's remark about the erotic function of the veil seems to be more a repetition of the rhetoric of inaccessibility that we find in orientalist romances of the eighteenth century than a statement about the role of voyeurism in human sexuality.

15   I am referring here to Lacan's statement in "Subversion du sujet et dialectique du désir dans l'inconscient freudian": "le désir est une défense, défense d'outre passer une limite dans la jouissance" (*Écrits*, 188). The veil's symbolic function, as a representation of castration, is to make the subject recognize the *manque* that governs his desire. Lacan finishes the essay by stating that "la castration veut dire qu'il faut que la jouissance soit refusée, pour qu'elle puisse être atteinte sur l'échelle renversée de la Loi du désir" (199).

16   Said, *Orientalism*, p. 158.

17   Nerval, of course, obtained most of his information about the harem from William Lane's *Modern Egyptians*, which he consulted and copied substantially in composing "Les femmes du Caire." In *Voyageurs et écrivains français en Egypte*, Carré reproduces Sainte Fare Garnot's outline of Nerval's borrowings from Lane.

18   Michel Foucault, *L'ordre du discours* (Paris: Gallimard, 1971).

2. From Travelogue to Tourist Guide:
The Orientalist as Sightseer

1   As a *touriste*, Nerval also distances himself from Orientalism as an *intertextual practice* linked to a protected and grand mode of traveling which prevents the traveler from contact with a "reality" defined here as poverty and deprivation—note Nerval's frequent uses of *sans*. I cannot do a close reading of this passage to point out its ambivalences, but for an illuminating discussion of it, see Ross Chambers, "Voyage et écriture: le premier chapitre du *Voyage en Orient*," *Cahiers de la Société Gérard de Nerval* 8 (1985):21–25.

2   Jean-Claude Berchet, Introduction, *Le Voyage en Orient* (Paris: Robert Laffont, 1985), 10. I also consulted Daniel J. Boorstin, *The Image* (New York: Atheneum, 1975), 77–117, for my discussion of the rise of tourism in Europe.

3   Of course, Nerval's *Voyage en Orient* uses the intertextual allusion to guidebooks as a way of distinguishing itself from its own travelogue predecessors—e.g., Chateaubriand's *Itinéraire de Paris à Jérusalem* and Lamartine's *Voyage en Orient*.

My use of the term *discursive formation* is derived from Michel Foucault's discussion of discursive regularities in *L'Archéologie du savoir* (Paris: Editions Gallimard, 1969). Foucault uses the term to describe the "system of dispersion" in the statements of a discourse—e.g., medicine, grammar, political economy—and the regularities between its objects, functionings, concepts, etc. All quoted passages from this text are from A. M. Sheridan Smith's translation, *The Archaeology of Knowledge and The Discourse on Language* (New York: Pantheon Books, 1972).

4 "Une sorte d'euphorie toute fraîche à *acheter* l'effort, à en garder l'image et la vertu sans en subir le malaise" from Roland Barthes, *Mythologies* (Paris: Points-Editions du Seuil, 1957; New York: Hill and Wang, 1983), pp. 122 and 74, respectively.

5 "Le *Guide Bleu* témoigne de la vanité de toute description analytique, celle qui refuse à la fois l'explication et la phénoménologie" (Barthes, *Mythologies*, 123).

6 Dean MacCannell, *The Tourist: A New Theory of the Leisure Class* (New York: Schocken Books, 1976); Jonathan Culler, "Semiotics of Tourism," *American Journal of Semiotics* 1.1–2 (1981):127–40; also see Nelson H. H. Graburn, "Tourism: The Sacred Journey," in *Hosts and Guests: The Anthropology of Tourism*, ed. V. Smith (Philadelphia: University of Pennsylvania Press, 1977).

7 Susan Buck-Morss, "Semiotic Boundaries and the Politics of Meaning: Modernity on Tour. A Village in Transition," in *New Ways of Knowing: The Sciences, Society, and Reconstructive Knowledge*, ed. Marcus G. Raskin and Herbert J. Bernstein (Newark, N.J.: Rowman and Littlefield, 1987), 203; Dennison Nash, "Tourism as a Form of Imperialism," in Smith, *Hosts and Guests*, 33–47; see also Davydd J. Greenwood, "Culture by the Pound: An Anthropological Perspective in Tourism as Cultural Commoditization," in Smith, *Hosts and Guests*, 129–38.

8 Following Foucault's use of this term, *enunciative modalities* means all the attributes and propositions that define the role of the speaking subject, varying from autobiographical data to qualitative descriptions of the speaker. I will discuss these in more detail later, when I compare the tourist guide with the travelogue.

9 Cf. James Buzard, "A Continent of Pictures: Reflections on the 'Europe' of Nineteenth-Century Tourists," *PMLA* 108.1 (1992):30–44.

10 Richard Burton, *Personal Narrative of a Pilgrimage to El-Medinah and Meccah* (New York: G. P. Putnam, 1856), 17.

11 Volney, *Voyage en Syrie et en Egypte*, 22.

12 In his discussion of the "formations of strategies," Foucault points out that every discursive formation in its theoretical choices depends on an authority that is characterized by the "possible positions of desire in relation to discourse [se caractérise par les positions possibles du désir par rapport au discours]" (90).

13 The dispersion of the speaking subject, one may argue, also corresponds to the dispersion of power in the nineteenth century, which has been elucidated by Foucault in *Surveiller et punir* (Paris: Editions Gallimard, 1975); see in particular his discussion of panoptism (197–230).

14 Murray, *Hand-Book for Travellers in the Ionian Islands, Greece, Turkey, Asia Minor, and Constantinople* (London: John Murray, 1840), iv.

15   Walter Benjamin, *Illuminations* (New York: Schocken Books, 1969), 89.

16   Roland Barthes, *S/Z* (Paris: Points-Editions du Seuil, 1970), 85.

17   The accumulative overproduction of detail produces also a sense of history, transforming the tourist's synchronic vision into a diachronic "depth vision" that perceives significance rather than merely brute matter. In this sense, the guide resembles the travelogue in engaging in acts of interpretation.

18   Fabian, *Time and the Other*, 106.

19   See James Clifford, "On Ethnographic Authority," in *Predicament of Culture*, 21–54. The quotation is from Said, *Orientalism*, 5.

20   Daniel Boorstin mentions that the rise of tourism was also attacked in England by "sophisticated Englishmen" such as John Ruskin, who complained about Cook's tours to the Holy Land and other parts of the world. See *The Image*, 87.

21   Pierre Loti, *La Mort de Philae* (Paris: Galmann-Lévy, 1908), 8, 17–30. My attention was drawn to this text by Berchet's introduction to *Le Voyage en Orient*.

22   Buck-Morss, "Semiotic Boundaries and the Politics of Meaning," 218.

3. Notes on Notes, or with Flaubert in Paris, Egypt

1   When I speak of Flaubert's *Notes de voyages*, I have in mind three texts. First, I mean the original *Carnets de Notes de voyages* that make up Flaubert's original notebooks, in which he recorded his impression of the journey *sur place* during 1849–50—specifically here carnets 4 and 5, which contain the notes taken during his Egyptian trip. Second, I am referring to the rewritten notes that are often published as part of Flaubert's complete works. These were first published in 1925 by René Descharmes in Edition du Centaire, but I use Maurice Bardeche's edition (Paris: Club be l'Honnête Homme, 1974), vol. 10. Third, I mean Flaubert's letters from Egypt to his mother and to Louis Bouilhet and a few other friends. I use Antoine Youssef Naaman's *Les Lettres D'Egypt de Gustave Flaubert* (Paris: Nizet, 1965). All page references are given parenthetically in the text.

2   The notion of belated Orientalism, as I suggest in the Introduction, is not chronological but ideological. That is to say, belated Orientalism does not hold a temporal relation to other modes of orientalist discourse—romantic Orientalism (e.g., Lamartine and Chateaubriand), (pseudo)scientific Orientalism (e.g., Volney and Savary), Victorian Orientalism (e.g., Burton and Doughty), etc.—but a conceptual relation that differentiates it from them. Throughout my notes I try to delineate this differential relation by describing the fragmentary elements of belated Orientalism.

3   Flaubert states his lack of interest in publishing anything on the Orient in a letter to Doctor Cloquet, a close family friend (see Naaman, *Lettres*, 174). I use the word *perverse* in this sentence in both its Freudian sense of sexual perversion and following my earlier use meaning "split." For a psychoanalytic discussion of Flaubert's perversity in the Orient, see Dennis Porter, "The Perverse Traveler: Flaubert's *Voyage en Orient*," *L'Esprit Créateur* 24.1 (Spring 1989):24–36.

4   I borrow this term from Richard Terdiman, to whose discussion of "corrosive

intertextuality" in Flaubert my essay is indebted. See his "Ideological Voyages: On a Flaubertian Dis-Orient-ation," in *Discourse/Counter-discourse* (Ithaca: Cornell University Press, 1985), 227–60.

5   My notion of interpretive drift is based on Roland Barthes's discussion of *dérive* as a source of textual pleasure in *Le plaisir du texte*, 32–33.

6   Cf. ibid., 46–49.

7   I cannot avoid the fact that this kind of writing provokes contradictory responses. Consider the following responses of my readers to an earlier version of this chapter. One reader found it " 'cute' to adopt a purported note form, when in fact [I] end up providing long sections of text on different topics which emerge as having a 'logical' sequence of their own." Another reader thought that "what seems interesting about writing [this chapter] in fragments is that the categories are neither hierarchized in terms of importance nor organized in terms of chronology, i.e., the narrative of an argument."

8   In the second version of his notes, Flaubert transforms the phrase "silence du désert" into "—silence.—silence.—silence."

9   Cf. Susan Stewart, "Objects of Desire," in *On Longing* (Baltimore: Johns Hopkins University Press, 1984), 132–69.

10   Needless to say, the displacement of the souvenir object serves as the signifier of the possessor's "power" over the Orient.

11   Charles Lapierre, *Esquisse sur Flaubert Intime* (Paris: Evreux Charles Hérissey, 1898), 5–6.

12   His fourth letter to Louis Bouilhet says, "Je m'en vais te faire une confidence très nette—c'est que je ne m'occupe pas plus de ma mission que du roi de Prusse. Pour remplir mon mandat exactement il eût fallu renoncer à mon voyage" (*Lettres*, 279).

13   In the original notes, Flaubert points out that he was told, "She is a little crazy, Sir!"

14   Cf. Julia Kristeva, *Pouvoirs de l'horreur* (Paris: Editions du Seuil, 1980).

15   The bibliographic card for Flaubert's carnet 4 states: "The manuscript contains passages that decency prevents us from publishing."

16   Flaubert begins his *Notes* with the sad account of his departure from Croisset, describing his mother's violent crying and then his own depression—"I closed the windows (I was alone), and hold my handkerchief on my mouth and started crying" (435)—and ends the chronicle of his Egyptian tour with several references to his profound sense of "tristesse du départ" (549).

17   Cf. Julia Kristeva, *Soleil noir: Dépression et mélancolie* (Paris: Gallimard, 1987), 11–43.

4. Kipling's "Other" Narrator/Reader: Self-Exoticism and the Micropolitics of Colonial Ambivalence

1   I call myself a "postcolonial" viewer to emphasize that my position as a viewer of these colonialist photographs—and later as a reader of the colonialist texts of Kipling—is a particular historical position that allows me to read and locate the splits and ambivalences in them. The recognition of such positionality is meant to ac-

knowledge the danger of conflating the different responses at different historical junctures to the colonial encounter, hoping to avoid the problematic tendency to represent colonialism by the semiotic of postcoloniality.

I borrow the Latin term *studium,* and later *punctum,* from Roland Barthes's discussion of photography in *Camera Lucida,* trans. Richard Howard (New York: Hill and Wang, 1983); [*La chambre claire* (Paris: Editions de l'Etoile, Gallimard, Le Seuil, 1980)]. Barthes uses the first term to mean a "general enthusiastic commitment," a "field of cultural interest" that a photograph communicates to the viewer through its intended message (226, 94). The second term connotes a particular detail in the photograph that "pricks" the viewer by exposing to him or her a "subtle *beyond*" of the photographer's coded message.

2   As will become apparent in my discussion in this chapter, mediation is split in several ways. To begin, the native mediates the British colonizer's identity as master. But by virtue of that mediation, the colonized native also mediates the master's identity, differentially defined as "exotic"—leading *à la limite* to identification with the British lady's "coolie" or in going "native." The phenomenon of English self-exoticism itself mediates, for postcolonial readers, the presence and identity of the colonized natives, the subjectivity that is repressed when it is produced as Other and as mediator, both of which are the excluded third in the colonial communication system. And finally, I try to show how this thematic system of existential identity is replicated discursively on a micropolitical level in the self-exoticism of Kipling's writing.

3   Mikhail Bakhtin, "Discourse in the Novel," in *The Dialogic Imagination,* ed. Michael Holquist, trans. Caryl Emerson and Michael Holquist (Austin: University of Texas Press, 1981). I will discuss the phenomenon of heteroglossia in greater detail later in this chapter.

4   The quotations are from George Orwell, but the ideas have been expressed by most of Kipling's readers; see Orwell, "Rudyard Kipling," in *Kipling and the Critics,* ed. Elliot Gilbert (New York: New York University Press, 1965), 76. Indeed, since Oscar Wilde and Max Beerbohm began ridiculing his fiction in the late nineteenth century, Kipling has always been read and condemned in terms of his colonial message. Only recently have such critics as Abdul JanMohamed ("The Economy of Manichean Allegory: The Function of Racial Difference in Colonialist Literature," in Gates, ed., *"Race," Writing, and Difference*), John McClure (*Kipling and Conrad: The Colonial Fiction* [Cambridge: Harvard University Press, 1981]), and Zohreh Sullivan ("Kipling the Nightwalker," in *Rudyard Kipling,* ed. Harold Bloom [New York: Chelsea House, 1987]) begun to study the complexities of Kipling's colonialist representation.

5   My discussion of ideological ambivalence as a sign of the productivity of colonial authority is indebted to Homi Bhabha's insightful and provocative discussion of this issue. See, for example, "Signs Taken for Wonders: Questions of Ambivalence and Authority under a Tree Outside Delhi, May 1817," in Gates, ed., *"Race," Writing, and Difference,* 163–84; and also "The Other Question: Difference, Discrimination and the Discourse of Colonialism."

6   Cf. Lacan's "The Subject and the Other: Alienation," in *The Four Fundamental Concepts of Psycho-Analysis* (New York: W. W. Norton, 1977) [*Le Séminaire de Jacques Lacan, Livre 11, Les quatre concepts fondamentaux de psychanalyse* (Paris: Editions du Seuil, 1973)].

7   Kipling actually wrote two pieces under this title. One is the narrative of his long personal journey to the depths of the city of Calcutta in which he narrates his descent from "A Real Live City" all the way to the lowest circle of "hell," where he visits an opium factory. The other is a short sketch of Lahore, in which the more "imaginative" narrator wanders around the town as a *flâneur*. Here I will discuss mostly the second piece, though most of what I say can be traced in the first narrative as well.

8   Rudyard Kipling, *Life's Handicap* (New York: Oxford University Press, 1987), 270. Unless otherwise indicated, all my references are to this edition. Page references are given parenthetically in the text, using the abbreviations LH (*Life's Handicap*) and PTH (*Plain Tales from the Hills*).

9   The Simla Club as a whole symbolizes the colonizer's attempt to overcome his anxieties by regressing into a familiar and comfortable world. The club, as John McClure suggests, is a "little solace," providing the colonizer with a "false security" of home (McClure, *Kipling and Conrad*, 37).

10   It is suggestive that Pluffles's Colonel "chuckled when he heard of the education of Pluffles [i.e., his affair with Mrs. Reiver] and said it was a good training for the boy" (pp. 44–45). John McClure has explained that abandonment and humiliation were viewed by the imperial system as an important part of the colonizer's education, because it is precisely the terror of isolation and the fear of alienation that make the exercise of authority effective. The more alienated the colonizer, the better he or she follows authority and the better she or he serves the interests of the empire.

11   Strickland, whose unconventional methods of policing include disguising himself as a native servant, is a familiar character in Kipling's Anglo-Indian stories, among them "Miss Youghal's Sais," "The Bronckhorst Divorce-Case," "The Mark of the Beast," "The Return of Imray," and "A Deal in Cotton."

12   Mikhail Bakhtin, "Discourse in the Novel," 313.

13   *In Black and White* (New York: Aldus Edition De Luxe, 1909), 7:217 [hereafter B&W]. All page references for the stories in this collection are from this edition and are given parenthetically in the text.

14   The words are Bhabha's ("The Other Question"). He uses them to problematize Edward Said's notion of power and knowledge as being possessed only by the colonizer.

5. Colonial Ethnography and the Politics of Gender: The Everyday Life of an Orientalist Journey

1   Gustave Flaubert, *Correspondance*, vol. 1 (Paris: Bibliothèque de la Plèiade, 1973), 663.

2   Chris Bongie, *Exotic Memories: Literature, Colonialism, and the Fin de Siècle*.

3   Mary Louise Pratt, "Fieldwork in Common Places," in *Writing Culture: The Poetics and*

Politics of Ethnography, ed. James Clifford and George E. Marcus (Berkeley: University of California Press, 1986), 27–50.

4 Billie Melman, *Women's Orient: English Women and the Middle East, 1718–1918* (Ann Arbor: University of Michigan Press, 1992).

5 Lady Anne Blunt, *A Pilgrimage to Nejd: The Cradle of the Arab Race*, 2 vols. (London: Frank Cass, 1968), 1:62. The travelogue was originally published by John Murray in 1881. All page references are given parenthetically in the text.

6 Victor Segalen, *Essai sur l'exotisme: Une esthétique du Divers* (Montpellier: Fata Morgana, 1978).

7 See Melman, *Women's Orient*, 286.

8 James Clifford, "On Ethnographic Authority," in *Predicament of Culture*, 31.

9 Johannes Fabian, *Time and the Other*, see in particular chapter 4, "The Other and the Eye: Time and the Rhetoric of Vision."

10 Clifford, in *Writing Culture*, 98–121.

11 Mary Louise Pratt, *Imperial Eyes: Travel Writing and Transculturation* (New York: Routledge, 1992), 201–8.

12 Behdad, "The Eroticized Orient: Images of the Harem in Montesquieu and His Precursors," *Stanford French Review* 13.2–3 (Fall–Winter 1989):109–26.

13 *Proceedings of the Royal Geographical Society and Monthly Record of Geography* 2 (February 1880):100, 102.

6. Allahou Akbar! He Is a Woman: Colonialism, Transvestism, and the Orientalist Parasite

1 To my knowledge, there is no nonbiographical work on Eberhardt's writing. Even theoretical works about her, such as Denise Brahimi's *L'oued et la zaouïa: Lectures d'Isabelle Eberhardt* (Algiers: Office des Publications Universitaires, 1983); Laura Rice's " 'Nomad Thought': Isabelle Eberhardt and the Colonial Project," *Cultural Critique* 17 (Winter 1990–91):151–76; and Marjorie Garber's "The Chic of Araby: Transvestism and the Erotics of Cultural Appropriation," in *Vested Interests: Cross-Dressing and Cultural Anxiety* (New York: Harper Perennial, 1992), 304–52, present their arguments through recourse to biographic details.

2 Garber, "Chic of Araby," 328.

3 In this respect, I agree with both Michel Foucault and Roland Barthes in their critique of privileging the author as a point of origin. See Foucault, "What Is an Author?" in *Language, Counter-memory, Practice*, ed. Donald F. Bouchard, (Ithaca: Cornell University Press, 1977), 113–38; and Roland Barthes, "The Death of the Author," in *Image, Music, Text*, trans. Stephen Heath (New York: Hill and Wang, 1977), 142–48.

4 Cf. Vincent Pecora, "What was Deconstruction?" *Contention* 1.3 (Spring 1992): 59–80.

5 My reading of Eberhardt's texts through her biography does *not* imply that I consider biographical discourse a more "truthful" mode of representation than, say,

fiction. On the contrary, I am critical of biographical discourse's "referential fallacy" and treat it as a kind of story telling that can be helpful in reading an autobiographical text such as Eberhardt's.

6 Kaja Silverman's essay "White Skin, Brown Masks: The Double Mimesis, or with Lawrence in Arabia," *Differences* 1.3 (Fall 1989):3–54, has been an inspiring text in my attempt to contextualize Eberhardt's journey in North Africa.

7 In this sense, Eberhardt's writing parallels Nerval's and Flaubert's, which I discuss in previous chapters.

8 I have consulted several biographic accounts of Eberhardt's life to tell this story of her involvement in North Africa, without, of course, wanting to claim a transsubjective or ideological authority for my narrative. Annette Kobak's *Isabelle: The Life of Isabelle Eberhardt* (New York: Vintage Books, 1988) has been the most helpful text to my argument. I also used Marie-Odile Delacour and Jean-René Huleu, *Sables, Le roman de la vie d'Isabelle Eberhardt* (Paris: Editions Liana Levi, 1986); and Françoise D'Eaubonne, *La Couronne de sable* (Paris: Flammarion, 1967), in writing the following biographic account.

9 Eberhardt constantly cites Loti's works in her *Journaliers*, which indicates the extent of her admiration for the orientalist. One also encounters many of Loti's themes in her writing, among which Oriental melancholia and the image of the Orient as a locus of personal liberation are striking.

10 Isabelle is almost always referred to as a "wild" woman. Her passion for "promiscuous" sexual relations with sailors and Arab men made her a popular topic of gossip among the French colonizers, who seem to have been seriously threatened by her relations with North African men. Such relationships crossed the racial and cultural boundaries on which colonial authority depended.

11 Isabelle Eberhardt, *Oeuvres complètes. Écrits sur le sable*, vol. 1, ed. Marie-Odile Delacour and Jean-René Huleu (Paris: Grasset, 1988), 44, 47. All page references given parenthetically in the text are to this edition.

12 A Spahi was a native North African who had joined the colonial army and adopted French citizenship. Spahis were often resented by the native population.

13 For a discussion of this issue, see Hélène Cixous, "Le Rire de la Médusa," *L'Arc* 61 (1975):39–54.

14 For a provocative discussion of colonial mimicry, see Homi Bhabha, "Of Mimicry and Man: The Ambivalence of Colonial Discourse," *October* 28 (Spring 1984):125–33.

15 The notion of transculturation has its genesis in Cuban poet Nancy Morejón's discussion of the symbolic and social exchanges among various cultures that interact with each other; see her *Nación y mestizaje en Nicolás Guillé* (Havana: Union, 1982). But my use of this notion is mediated by Françoise Lionnet's and Mary Louis Pratt's useful rearticulations of this concept; see, respectively, "Logiques Métisses: Cultural Appropriation and Postcolonial Representations," *College Literature* 19.3 (October 1992) and 20.1 (February 1993):100–120; and *Imperial Eyes: Travel Writing and Transculturation* (New York: Routledge, 1992).

16 For a fascinating discussion of the relation between gender and masquerade, see Joan Riviere, "Womanliness as Masquerade," in *Formations of Fantasy*, ed. Victor Burgin, James Donald, and Cora Kaplan (London: Metheuen, 1986), 35–44.

17 Of course, Eberhardt's identification with the male Oriental is both ironic and symptomatic because the Orient and its inhabitants, as Edward Said has demonstrated, are "feminized" by the West, which makes her attempt to go beyond the predicaments of being a woman problematic. That she denies her Western femininity to identify with a feminized "Oriental masculinity" is symptomatic of her marginal position as a woman who even in attempting to go beyond the social limitations of her gender replicates that very same marginality.

18 Requoted from Kabak's *Isabelle*, 198. Needless to say, the quotation is a telling statement about the duplicitous nature of "liberal" attitudes of people such as Barrucand, who managed to work for the empire while claiming to be sympathetic to Arabs.

19 For a historical account of this shift, see Raymond F. Betts, *Assimilation and Association in French Colonial Theory 1890–1914* (New York: Columbia University Press, 1961).

"Tristesse du Depart": An Open-ended Conclusion

1 Renato Rosaldo, *Culture and Truth: The Remaking of Social Analysis* (Boston: Beacon Press, 1989), 68–90.

2 Bhabha, "Signs Taken for Wonders," 172.

3 Tweeds's catalog is in this respect an interesting example of how ordinary shopping becomes an activity for expressing a desire for the Orient that is simultaneously produced by and productive of orientalist images and stereotypes.

4 Foucault, *Power/Knowledge*, 99.

5 Gayatri Spivak, *The Post-colonial Critic*, ed. Sarah Harasym (New York: Routledge, 1990), 95–112.

6 Ibid., 105. As Spivak herself admits, this analogy is not perfect; operations, as one knows, don't prevent people from dying in the end either, for they are also a form of maintenance and remain open-ended. But the idea of daily maintenance as an analogy for the practice of open-ended criticism is useful nonetheless.

7 I have argued elsewhere that postcolonial teachers and intellectuals in the academy ought to look more carefully at their micropractices. If, as "specific intellectuals," postcolonial teachers and theoreticians are to play a crucial part in the general functioning of the apparatus of truth in the neocolonial era, this general function has to work out of the specific position these intellectuals occupy in the cultural space of the academy. See my "Traveling to Teach: Postcolonial Critics in the American Academy," in *Race, Identity and Representation in Education*, ed. Cameron McCarthy and Warren Crichlow (New York: Routledge, 1993).

8 Bhabha, "The Other Question," 149.

Bibliography

✾

Abbot, Paul. "On Authority." *Screen* 20.2 (1979):11–64.

Abdel Malek, Anwar. "Orientalism en Crise." *Diogène* 24 (1963):109–42.

Ageron, Charles-Robert. *L'Anticolonialisme en France de 1871 à 1914*. Paris: Presses Universitaires de France, 1973.

Ahmad, Aijaz. *In Theory: Classes, Nations, Literatures*. London: Verso, 1992.

Alloula, Malek. *Le harem colonial: Images d'un sous-érotisme*. Trans. Myrna and Wald Godzich as *The Colonial Harem*. Minneapolis: University of Minnesota Press, 1986.

Althusser, Louis. *Lenin and Philosophy and Other Essays*. Trans. Ben Brester. London: NLB, 1971.

Asad, Talal, ed. *Anthropology and the Colonial Encounter*. London: Ithaca Press, 1975.

Bakhtin, Mikhail. *The Dialogic Imagination*. Ed. Michael Holquist. Austin: University of Texas Press, 1981.

Ballhatchet, Kenneth. *Race, Sex, and Class under the Raj: Imperial Attitudes and Policies and Their Critics, 1793–1905*. New York: St. Martin's Press.

Barker, Francis, Peter Hulme, Margaret Iversen, and Diana Loxley, eds. *Europe and Its Others*. 2 vols. Clochester: University of Essex Press, 1985.

———. *Literature, Politics and Theory: Papers from the Essex Conference*. London: Methuen, 1986.

———. *Politics of Theory*. Clochester: University of Essex Press, 1983.

Barrès, Maurice. *Une enquête aux pays du Levant*. Paris: Plon Nourrit, 1923.

Barthes, Roland. *La chambre claire*. Paris: Edition de l'Etoile, Gallimard, Le Seuil, 1980.

———. *Image, Music, Text*. Trans. Stephen Heath. New York: Hill and Wang, 1977.

———. *Mythologies*. Paris: Editions du Seuil, 1957.

———. *Le plaisir du texte*. Paris: Editions du Seuil, 1973.

———. *Roland Barthes*. Paris: Editions du Seuil, 1975.

———. *S/Z*. Paris: Editions du Seuil, 1970.

Behdad, Ali. "The Eroticized Orient: Images of the Harem in Montesquieu and His Precursors." *Stanford French Review* 13.2–3 (1989):109–26.

———. "Traveling to Teach: Third-World Critics in the American Academy." In *Race, Identity, and Representation in Education*, ed. Cameron McCarthy and Warren Crichlow. New York: Routledge, 1993.

Benjamin, Walter. *Charles Baudelaire: A Lyric Poet in the Era of High Capitalism*. Trans. Harry Zohn. London: New Left Books, 1973.

———. *Illuminations*. Ed. Hannah Arendt. New York: Schocken Books, 1969.

Berchet, Jean-Claude, ed. Introduction to *Le Voyage en Orient*. Paris: Robert Laffont, 1985.

Betts, Raymond. *Assimilation and Association in French Colonial Theory, 1890–1914*. New York: Columbia University Press, 1961.

Bhahba, Homi. "Of Mimicry and Man: The Ambivalence of Colonial Discourse." *October* 28 (Spring 1984):125–33.

———. "The Other Question: Difference, Discrimination and the Discourse of Colonialism." In *Literature, Politics & Theory: Papers from the Essex Conference*, ed. F. Barker et al., 148–72. London: Methuen, 1986.

———. "Signs Taken for Wonders: Questions of Ambivalence and Authority under a Tree Outside Delhi, May 1817." In *"Race," Writing, and Difference*, ed. H. L. Gates, Jr., 163–84. Chicago: University of Chicago Press.

Blunt, Lady Anne. *Journals and Correspondence, 1878–1917*. Ed. Rosemary Archer and James Fleming. Cheltenham, Gloucestershire: Alexander Heriot, 1986.

———. *A Pilgrimage to Nejd: The Cradle of the Arab Race*. 2 vols. London: Frank Cass, 1968.

Bongie, Chris. *Exotic Memories: Literature, Colonialism, and the Fin de Siècle*. Stanford: Stanford University Press, 1991.

Boorstin, Daniel. *The Image*. New York: Atheneum, 1975.

Bouhdiba, Abdelwahab. *La sexualité en Islam*. Paris: Quadrige/Presses Universitaires de France, 1986.

Bourdieu, Pierre. *Outline of a Theory of Practice*. Cambridge: Cambridge University Press, 1977.

Brahimi, Denise. *L'oued et la zaouïa: Lectures d'Isabelle Eberhardt*. Algiers: Office des Publications Universitaires, 1983.

Bruneau, Jean. *Le "Conte Oriental" de Flaubert*. Paris: Denoel, 1973.

Buck-Morss, Susan. "Semiotic Boundaries and the Politics of Meaning: Modernity on Tour. A Village in Transition." In *New Ways of Knowing: The Sciences, Society, and Reconstructive Knowledge*, ed. Marcus Raskin and Herbert Bernstein, 200–236. Newark, N.J.: Rowman and Littlefield, 1987.

Burton, Sir Richard. *Personal Narrative of a Pilgrimage to El-Medinah and Meccah*. New York: G. P. Putnam, 1856.

Butor, Michael. *Improvisations sur Flaubert*. Paris: Editions de la Difference, 1984.

———. "Le voyage et l'écriture." In *Repertoire IV*. Paris: Editions de Minuit, 1971.

Buzard, James. "A Continent of Pictures: Reflections on the 'Europe' of Nineteenth-Century Tourists." *PMLA* 108. 1 (1992):30–44.

Calvino, Italo. *Invisible Cities*. Trans. William Weaver. New York: Harcourt Brace Jovanovich, 1972.

Carré, Jean-Marie. *Voyageurs et écrivains français en Egypte.* 2 vols. Cairo: Imprimerie de l'Institut Français d'Archéologie Orientale, 1956.

Césaire, Aimé. *Discours sur le colonialisme.* Paris: Présence Africaine, 1962.

Chambers, Ross. *Gérard de Nerval et la Poétique du voyage.* Paris: José Corti, 1969.

———. "Voyage et écriture: le premier chapitre du *Voyage en Orient.*" *Cahiers de la Société Gérard de Nerval* 8 (1985): 21–25.

———. *Mélancolie et opposition: Les débuts du modernisme en France.* Paris: José Corti, 1987.

———. *Room for Maneuver: Reading (the) Opposition (in) Narrative.* Chicago: University of Chicago Press, 1991.

Chateaubriand, François-René. *Itinéraire de Paris à Jérusalem.* Ed. Jean Mourot. Paris: Garnier-Flammarion, 1968.

Clifford, James. "Notes on Theory and Travel." *Inscriptions* 5 (1989): 177–88.

———. *The Predicament of Culture: Twentieth-Century Ethnography, Literature, and Art.* Cambridge: Harvard University Press, 1988.

———. "Traveling Cultures." In *Cultural Studies,* ed. Lawrence Grossberg, Cary Nelson, and Paula Treichler, 96–112. New York: Routledge, 1992.

Clifford, James, and George Marcus, eds. *Writing Culture: The Poetics and Politics of Ethnography.* Berkeley: University of California Press, 1986.

Coetzee, J. M. *White Writing: On Culture of Letters in South Africa.* New Haven: Yale University Press, 1988.

Comaroff, Jean. *Body of Power, Spirit of Resistance.* Chicago: University of Chicago Press, 1985.

Culler, Jonathan. "Semiotics of Tourism." *American Journal of Semiotics* 1.1–2 (1981): 127–40.

Daniel, Norman. *Islam, Europe and Empire.* Edinburgh: Edinburgh University Press, 1966.

D'Eaubonne, Françoise. *La Couronne de sable.* Paris: Flammarion, 1967.

De Certeau, Michel. *The Practice of Everyday Life.* Berkeley: University of California Press, 1984.

———. "Writing vs. Time: History and Anthropology in the Works of Lafitau." *Yale French Studies* 59 (1980): 37–64.

Delacour, Marie-Odile, and Jean-Réne Huleu. *Sables, Le roman de la vie d'Isabelle Eberhardt.* Paris: Editions Liana Levi, 1986.

Derrida, Jacques. *De la grammatologie.* Paris: Editions de Minuit, 1967.

———. *L'écriture et la différence.* Paris: Editions du Seuil, 1967.

Djaït, Hichem. *L'Europe et l'Islam.* Paris: Collection Esprit/Seuil, 1978.

Dugat, Gustave. *Histoire des orientalistes de l'Europe de XIIᵉ au XIXᵉ siècle.* 2 vols. Paris: Adrien Maisonneuve, 1868–70.

Eberhardt, Isabelle. *Oeuvres complètes.* 2 vols. Ed. Marie-Odile Delacour and Jean-René Huleu. Paris: Grasset, 1988.

Edwards, Michael. *Bound to Exile: The Victorians in India.* London: Sidgwick and Jackson, 1969.

El Nouty, Hassan. *Le Proche-Orient dans la littérature française de Nerval à Barrès.* Paris: Librairie Nizet, 1958.

Etienne, Monna, and Eleanor Leacock. *Women and Colonization.* New York: Praeger, 1980.

Fabian, Johannes. *Time and the Other: How Anthropology Makes Its Object.* New York: Columbia University Press, 1983.

Fanon, Frantz. *Peau noire, masques blancs.* Paris: Editions du Seuil, 1952.

Fellows, Sir Charles. *Travels and Researches in Asia Minor, more particularly in the Province of Lycia.* London: John Murray, 1852.

Feuchtwang, Stephen. "Socialist, Feminist, and Anti-Racist Struggles." m/f 4 (1980):41–56.

Flaubert, Gustave. *Correspondance.* Ed. Youssef Naaman. Paris: Nizet, 1965.

———. *Oeuvres complètes.* Ed. Maurice Bardeche. Paris: Club de l'Honnête Homme, 1973.

Foucault, Michel. *L'Archéologie du savoir.* Paris: Gallimard, 1969.

———. *Language, Counter-memory, Practice.* Ed. Donald Bouchard. Ithaca: Cornell University Press, 1977.

———. *L'Ordre du discours.* Paris: Gallimard, 1971.

———. *Power/Knowledge: Selected Interviews and Other Writings, 1972–1977.* Ed. Colin Gordon. New York: Pantheon Books, 1980.

———. *Surveiller et punir: Naissance de la prison.* Paris: Gallimard, 1975.

———. *La Volonté du savoir.* Paris: Gallimard, 1976.

Freud, Sigmund. *Three Essays on the Theory of Sexuality.* Trans. James Strachey. New York: Basic Books, 1962.

Garber, Marjorie. *Vested Interests: Cross-Dressing and Cultural Anxiety.* New York: Harper Perennial, 1992.

Gates, Henry Louis, Jr., ed. *"Race," Writing, and Difference.* Chicago: University of Chicago Press, 1986.

Geertz, Clifford. *The Interpretation of Cultures.* New York: Basic Books, 1973.

Gérard, René. *L'Orient et la pensée romantique allemande.* Paris: Didier, 1963.

Gilbert, Elliot, ed. *Kipling and the Critics.* New York: New York University Press, 1965.

Graburn, Nelson. "The Sacred Journey." In *Hosts and Guests: The Anthropology of Tourism*, ed. V. Smith, 17–31. Philadelphia: University of Pennsylvania Press, 1977.

Gramsci, Antonio. *The Prison Notebooks: Selections.* Trans. and ed. Quintin Hoare and Geoffrey Nowell Smith. New York: International Publishers, 1971.

Greenwood, Davydd. "Culture by Pound: An Anthropological Perspective in Tourism as Cultural Commoditization." In *Hosts and Guests: The Anthropology of Tourism*, ed. V. Smith, 129–38. Philadelphia: University of Pennsylvania Press, 1977.

Hentsch, Thierry. *L'Orient imaginaire: La vision politique occidentale de l'Est méditerranéen.* Paris: Editions de Minuit, 1988.

Hope, Thomas. *Anastasius, or, Memoirs of a Greek; written at the close of the Eighteenth Century.* London: John Murray, 1820.

Hourani, Albert. "Islam and the Philosophers of History." *Middle Eastern Studies* 3 (1967):204–68.

———. "Orientalism." *New York Review of Books* 8 (March 1979):29–30.

JanMohamed, Abdul. "The Economy of Manichean Allegory: The Function of Racial

Difference in Colonialist Literature." In *"Race," Writing, and Difference*, ed. H. L. Gates, Jr., 78–106. Chicago: University of Chicago Press, 1986.

Jeanneret, Michel. Introduction to *Voyage en Orient*, by Gérard de Nerval, 15–41. Paris: Garnier-Flammarion, 1980.

Jullian, Philippe. *Les Orientalistes: La vision de l'Orient par les peintres européens au XIXᵉ siècle*. Paris: Société française des Livres, 1977.

Kincaid, Dennis. *British Social Life in India, 1608–1937*. New York: Kennikat Press, 1971.

Kipling, Rudyard. *In Black and White*. New York: Aldus Edition De Luxe, 1909.

——. *The Day's Work*. New York: Oxford University Press, 1987.

——. *Kim*. New York: Oxford University Press, 1987.

——. *Life's Handicap*. New York: Oxford University Press, 1987.

——. *The Man Who Would Be King and Other Stories*. New York: Oxford University Press, 1987.

——. *Plain Tales from the Hills*. New York: Oxford University Press, 1987.

Kobak, Annette. *Isabelle: The Life of Isabelle Eberhardt*. New York: Vintage Books, 1988.

Kristeva, Julia. *Pouvoirs de l'horreur*. Paris: Editions du Seuil, 1980.

——. *Soleil noir: Dépression et mélancolie*. Paris: Gallimard, 1987.

Lacan, Jacques. *Écrits*. Paris: Editions du Seuil, 1971.

——. *Les Quatre concepts fondamentaux de psychanalyse*. Paris: Editions du Seuil, 1973.

Lamartine, Alphonse de. *Voyage en Orient*. Paris: Hachette, 1887.

Lane, Edward William. *An Account of the Manners and Customs of the Modern Egyptians*. London: J. M. Dent, 1936.

Lapierre, Charles. *Esquisse sur Flaubert Intime*. Paris: Evreux Charles Hérissey, 1898.

Laroui, Abdullah. *The History of Maghreb*. Trans. Ralph Manheim. Princeton: Princeton University Press, 1977.

Leclerc, Gérard. *Anthropologie et colonialisme*. Paris: Fayard, 1972.

Lionnet, Françoise. "Logiques Métisses: Cultural Appropriation and Postcolonial Representations." *College Literature* 19.3 (October 1992), 20.1 (February 1993):100–120.

Loti, Pierre. *Aziyadé*. Paris: Calmann-Lévy, 1879.

——. *Les Désenchantées*. Paris: Calmann-Lévy, 1906.

——. *Jérusalem*. Paris: Calmann-Lévy, 1895.

——. *La Mort de Philae*. Paris: Calmann-Lévy, 1908.

Lowe, Lisa. *Critical Terrains: French and British Orientalisms*. Ithaca: Cornell University Press, 1991.

Marchebeus. *Voyage de Paris à Constantinople par bateau à vapeur; nouvel itinéraire orné d'une carte et de cinquante vues et vignettes sur acier, avec tableaux indiquant les lieux desservis par les paquebots à vapeur, sur la méditerranée, l'Adriatique et le Danube, la prix des Places et des marchandises, les distances et la valeur des monnaies*. Paris: A. Bertrand, 1839.

Mbembe, Achille. "The Banality of Power and the Aesthetics of Vulgarity in the Postcolony." *Public Culture* 4.2 (Spring 1992):1–30.

McCannell, Dean. *The Tourist: A New Theory of the Leisure Class*. New York: Schocken Books, 1976.

McClure, John. *Kipling and Conrad: The Colonial Fiction*. Cambridge: Harvard University Press, 1981.

McKenna, Andrew. "Flaubert's Freudian Thing: Violence and Representation in *Salammbô*." *Stanford French Review* 12.2–3 (Fall–Winter 1988):305–26.

Melman, Billie. *Women's Orient: English Women and the Middle East, 1718–1918*. Ann Arbor: University of Michigan Press, 1992.

Moore-Gilbert, B. J. *Kipling and "Orientalism."* New York: St. Martin's Press, 1986.

Morejón, Nancy. *Nación y mestizaje en Nicolás Guillé*. Havana: Union, 1982.

Murray, John. *A Hand-Book for Travellers in the Ionian Islands, Greece, Turkey, Asia Minor, and Constantinople*. London: John Murray, 1840.

———. *A Hand-Book for Travellers in India and Pakistan, Burma and Ceylon*. 1859. Sixteenth ed., London: John Murray, 1949.

Nash, Dennison. "Tourism as a Form of Imperialism." In *Hosts and Guests: The Anthropology of Tourism*, ed. V. Smith, 33–47. Philadelphia: University of Pennsylvania Press, 1977.

Nerval, Gérard de. *Voyage en Orient*. 2 vols. Paris: Garnier-Flammarion, 1980.

Nochlim, Linda. "Imaginary Orient." *Art in America* 5 (1983):118–31, 187–91.

Orwell, George. "Rudyard Kipling." In *Kipling and the Critics*, ed. Elliot Gilbert, 74–87. New York: New York University Press, 1965.

Panikkar, K. M. *Asia and Western Dominance*. London: George Allen and Unwin, 1959.

Paulson, William. *The Noise of Culture: Literary Texts in a World of Information*. Ithaca: Cornell University Press, 1988.

Pecora, Vincent. "What Was Deconstruction?" *Contention* 1.3 (Spring 1992):59–80.

Porter, Dennis. "Orientalism and Its Problems." In *Politics of Theory*, ed. F. Barker et al., 179–93. Clochester: University of Essex Press, 1983.

———. "The Perverse Traveler: Flaubert's *Voyage en Orient*." *L'Esprit Créateur* 29.1 (Spring 1989): 24–36.

Pratt, Mary Louise. *Imperial Eyes: Travel Writing and Transculturation*. New York: Routledge, 1992.

Quetin. *Guide en Orient. Itinéraire scientique, artistique et pittoresque*. Paris: L. Maison, 1844.

———. *Guide du voyageur en Algérie. Itinéraire du savant, de l'artiste, de l'homme du monde et du colon*. Paris: L. Maison, 1846.

Rice, Laura. " 'Nomad Thought': Isabelle Eberhardt and the Colonial Project." *Cultural Critique* 17 (Winter 1990–91):151–76.

Richard, Jean-Pierre. "Géographie magique de Nerval." In *Poésie et Profondeur*. Paris: Editions du Seuil, 1955.

Rivet, Daniel. "L'âge d'or de l'orientalisme." *L'Histoire* 108 (February 1988):8–16.

Riviere, Joan. "Womanliness as Masquerade." In *Formations of Fantasy*, ed. Victor Burgin, James Donald, and Cora Kaplan. London: Methuen, 1986.

Rodinson, Maxime. *La Fascination de L'Islam*. Paris: Maspero, 1980.

———. "The Western Image and Western Studies of Islam." In *The Legacy of Islam*, ed. J. Schacht and C. E. Bosworth, 9–62. Oxford: Clarendon Press, 1974.

Rosaldo, Renato. *Culture and Truth: The Making of Social Analysis.* Boston: Beacon Press, 1989.

Said, Edward. *Beginnings: Intention and Method.* New York: Basic Books, 1975.

———. *Culture and Imperialism.* New York: Alfred A. Knopf, 1993.

———. "Identity, Authority, and Freedom: The Potentate and the Traveler." *Transition* 54 (1991): 4–18.

———. Interview in *Diacritics* 3 (1976): 30–47.

———. "Opponents, Audiences, Constituencies and Community." In *The Anti-Aesthetic: Essays on Postmodern Culture,* ed. Hal Foster, 135–59. Port Townsend, Wash.: Bay Press, 1983.

———. *Orientalism.* New York: Vintage Books, 1979.

———. "Orientalism Reconsidered." In *Literature, Politics and Theory,* ed. F. Barker et al., 210–29.

———. "The Politics of Knowledge." *Raritan* 11.1 (1991):17–31.

Schacht, Joseph, and C. E. Bosworth, eds. *The Legacy of Islam.* Oxford: Clarendon Press, 1974.

Schaeffer, Gérard. *Le voyage en Orient de Nerval: Études des structures.* Neuchâtel: La Baconnière, 1967.

Schwab, Raymond. *La Renaissance orientale.* Paris: Payot, 1950.

Segalen, Victor. *Essai sur l'exotisme. Une esthétique du Divers.* Montpellier: Fata Morgana, 1978.

Serres, Michel. *Le parasite.* Paris: Grasset, 1980.

Silverman, Kaja. "White Skin, Brown Masks: The Double Mimesis, or with Lawrence in Arabia." *Differences* 1.3 (1989):3–54.

Smith, Valene L., ed. *Hosts and Guests: The Anthropology of Tourism.* Philadelphia: University of Pennsylvania Press, 1977.

Spivak, Gayatri Chakravorty. *In Other Worlds: Essays in Cultural Politics.* New York: Methuen, 1987.

———. *The Post-colonial Critic: Interviews, Strategies, Dialogues.* Ed. Sarah Harasym. New York: Routledge, 1990.

Steegmuller, Francis, trans. and ed. *Flaubert in Egypt: A Sensibility on Tour.* Boston: Little, Brown, 1973.

Stewart, Susan. *On Longing: Narratives of the Miniature, the Gigantic, the Souvenir, the Collection.* Baltimore: Johns Hopkins University Press, 1984.

Sullivan, Zohreh. "Kipling the Nightwalker." In *Rudyard Kipling,* ed. Harold Bloom, 57–75. New York: Chelsea House, 1987.

Terdiman, Richard. *Discourse/Counter-discourse: The Theory and Practice of Symbolic Resistance in Nineteenth-Century France.* Ithaca: Cornell University Press, 1985.

Torgovnick, Marianna. *Gone Primitive: Savage Intellects, Modern Lives.* Chicago: University of Chicago Press, 1990.

Volney, Constantin-François. *Voyage en Egypte et en Syrie.* Ed. Jean Gaulmier. Paris: Mouton, 1959.

———. *Les ruines ou méditations sur les révolutions des empires.* Paris: Garnier, 1871.

Wetzel, Andreas. "Décrire l'Espagne: référent et réalité dans le récit de voyage littéraire."
    Stanford French Review 11.3 (Fall 1987): 359–73.

Williams, Raymond. *Culture and Society, 1780–1950.* New York: Harper and Row, 1966.

Wolf, Eric. *Europe and the People Without History.* Berkeley: University of California Press,
    1982.

Young, Robert. *White Mythologies: Writing History and the West.* New York: Routledge, 1990.

Index

Abjection, 66–68

Ahmad, Aijaz, 12–13

Ahmad, Eqbal, ix

Alienation, 77–78, 80–81, 84, 89, 147 n.10

All-Ahmad, Jalal, ix

Alloula, Malek: *The Colonial Harem*, 7–8

Althusser, Louis, 9; "Lenin and Philosophy," 2–4

Ambivalence: of colonial identity, 84, 125;
desire and, 33, 103; narrative framing
and, 85–86; of parasite, 114–15, 120;
production of, 89; productive nature
of, 77, 90–91, 110–11, 135, 146 n.5; of
traveler, 54

Anamnesia, 2, 6–8, 138; and amnesia, 47.
See also Belatedness; Postcolonialism

Anthropology: colonial encounter and, 6;
geography and, 101; Orientalism as
precursor to, 24, 46

Appropriation: circular relation of, 129;
colonial power and, 16; of difference,
112; of dominant discourse, 55; exoticism and, 85; of infinite space, 119; of
native voice, 85, 89–90; of Oriental
woman, 61; of Oriental signifiers, 123,
133; of the Other, 10–11, 14, 84

Authority (colonial), 94, 98; colonial

writers and, 88–89; production of, 30,
75, 77, 83, 140 n.16; and racial difference, 83, 91; splitting and, 91; tourist
guide and, 39, 43; travelogue and,
100

Bakhtin, Mikhail, 76, 86, 146 n.3

Barrès, Maurice, 48

Barrucand, Victor, 114, 127

Barthes, Roland, 18, 20, 45, 141 n.3, 145
n.5, 145–46 n.1 (chap. 4), 148 n.3; *Mythologies*, 36

Belatedness: authenticity of, 64; desire
and, 33, 43; of cultural transvestites, 59;
as oppositional praxis, 2, 7–9; of Orientalism, 54–55, 144 n.3; as politics of
contemporaneity, 9; as postcolonial
practice, 2–6; of postcolonial reader,
3–4, 76; quest for elsewhere and, 16,
33; of souvenir collector, 61; of travelers, 13–17, 54, 56, 63, 65–66, 70–72,
93, 116; will to discover and, 14, 47, 71,
92–93. *See also* Orientalism; Postcolonialism; Splitting

Benjamin, Walter, 43, 44

Berchet, Jean-Claude, 39

Betts, Raymond, 150 n.19

Ali Behdad is Assistant Professor of English and
Comparative Literature, University of California, Los
Angeles. He is the editor of *Orientalism* after *"Orientalism,"*
a special issue of *L'Esprit Créateur*, and the author of
several articles on post-colonial discourse.

Library of Congress Cataloging-in-Publication Data
Behdad, Ali, 1961 –
Belated travelers : orientalism in the age of colonial
dissolution / Ali Behdad.
p.   cm. — (Post-contemporary interventions)
Includes bibliographical references (p.   ) and index.
ISBN 0-8223-1454-1 (alk. paper). —
ISBN 0-8223-1471-1 (pbk. : alk. paper).
1. Orientalists.   2. Middle East—Foreign public
opinion, Occidental.   3. Middle East—Study and
teaching—Europe.   I. Title.   II. Series.
DS61.6.B44   1994
956—dc20   93-44399 CIP